THIS
BOOK
BELONGS TO

ACTIVE DRAMA

Active Drama is designed for middle secondary level to bridge the gap between the free-ranging 'creative drama' of the primary and early secondary years, with its strong emphasis on self-expression, and the high discipline of drama in Years 11 and 12.

The book analyses how drama works, demonstrates how to make it work, and provides ways to develop skills. Students are introduced to various non-verbal aspects of drama, and given practice in using these to bring life and meaning to printed words. Finally, all the elements are brought together in exercises in complete production scenes for performance.

ACTIVE DRAMA

Rosemary Lewis

HEINEMANN EDUCATIONAL AUSTRALIA

HEINEMANN EDUCATIONAL AUSTRALIA PTY LTD
85 Abinger Street, Richmond, Victoria 3121

First published 1981.
Designed and illustrated by Jonathan Waud

Typeset by Griffin Press Limited, Adelaide
Printed in Hong Kong by
Dah Hua Printing Press Co Ltd

Lewis, Rosemary
   Active drama.

   For secondary school students.
   ISBN 0 85859 244 4.

   1. Drama in education. I. Title.

792'.07'12

CONTENTS

INTRODUCTION

This is a practical book that analyses how drama works; demonstrates, in easy stages, how to make it work; and provides ways that develop skill in doing it.

The first section gives exercises to focus attention on those elements of drama which, because we use them continuously and unconsciously in our communication with others, we already use with skill. The exercises, based on personal experience, are extended by using them to bring text to life. The section begins with exercises to develop skills in participating in drama, and in constructing drama. These skills are then used in a structured way to develop drama from sources such as poetry and story. The third section gives practice in using the experience of drama that sections 1 and 2 have given, in bringing a drama text to life.

This book treats drama as a creative, imaginative, enjoyable activity, and as a discipline needing skill and understanding. In the practice of these two aspects of drama, the use of language is important. The exercises provide opportunities for discussion, and for finding the appropriate language for particular characters in particular contexts for particular purposes. The texts provide other voices to listen and respond to.

Two fine teachers have influenced my thinking about drama. Dorothy Heathcote's breakdown of the elements of drama into movement/stillness, silence/sound and light/dark removed the mystique from drama, making me see both the simplicity and the potential richness of it as a learning experience for an ordinary person. David Mallick's insistence on the necessity for excellence in the quality of English teaching has been inspirational. Without his support and questioning this book would not have been written.

The illustrations of Jonathan Waud, to whom I am indebted for helpful suggestions and additions in the movement work, widen the opportunities for response.

R L

ACKNOWLEDGEMENTS

The author and publishers would especially like to thank Jonathan Waud, whose suggestions for further practical work have been incorporated throughout the text.

The author and publishers would like to thank the following for permission to reproduce copyright material:

William Heinemann Ltd for extract from *West Side Story* by Arthur Laurents.

William Morris Agency for extract from *The Zoo Story* by Edward Albee.

Penguin Books Australia Ltd for 'I Saw A Man' from *Stockade* by Kenneth Cook.

Hope Leresche and Sayle Ltd for extract from *Oh What a Lovely War* by Charles Chiltern and Theatre Workshop. © 1965 by Joan Littlewood Productions Ltd.

Jonathan Cape Ltd and the Executors of the Ernest Hemingway Estate for 'The Killers' from *The First Forty-Nine Stories* by Ernest Hemingway.

The Bodley Head for *Dooley Is A Traitor* by James Michie.

David Higham Associates Ltd, the Trustees for the Copyright for the late Dylan Thomas, and J. M. Dent for extract from *Under Milkwood* by Dylan Thomas, and extract from *An Enemy of the People* (Act IV) by Henrik Ibsen (translator: Michael Meyer).

Currency Press Pty Ltd for 'Norm and Ahmed' from *Three Plays* by Alexander Buzo.

Queensland University Press for *Can't You Hear Me Talking To You* by Nora Dugon.

Faber & Faber Ltd for 'Act Without Words II: A Mime for Two Players' from *Breath and Other Shorts* by Samuel Beckett.

International Creative Management for extract from *Picnic* by William Inge.

Collier-Macmillan Australia for extract from *Spoon River Anthology* by Edward Lee Masters.

Heinemann Educational Australia for extract from *Move* by Bronwen Nicholls.

Every effort has been made to trace and contact owners of copyright material/copyright holders, but the publishers would be pleased to know of any errors or omissions.

Photograph Acknowledgements:

John O'Dwyer for photographs on p.4, p.5, p.6 (top 2), p.11 (bottom), p.16 (left side), p.18, p.21, p.68, p.69.

Sydney Morning Herald for photographs on p.11 (top).

John Fairfax and Sons Ltd for photograph on p.16 (rhs).

David Fenton (ED) SHOTS—the Underground Press, Academy Editions for photograph on p.72.

Northside Productions for photograph on page 22.

1 NON-VERBAL ELEMENTS OF DRAMA

When we enter a room for the first time, we may notice the way the furniture is arranged, the colour of the curtains, the kind of ornaments or the general condition of the room. This may lead us to make inferences about the use of the room (for public meetings? for parties? for eating?), or the life-style of the people who live or work in the room.

In the same way, we may notice different things about a person at our first meeting, and may react favourably or unfavourably before any words are spoken.

It is an old saying that actions speak louder than words. Your neighbour might say "Of course I don't mind your dog barking. It's the natural thing for a dog to do". Later that day you happen to see your neighbour turn the hose on your dog as it barks by the fence. What inferences might you make?

What experience can you recall when actions spoke louder than words?

What do you notice about a person you are meeting for the first time? How much can you tell about a person from dress? eyes? voice? How reliable are first impressions?

We shall begin by identifying and practising some of the ways in which we communicate without using words, for in drama we need to consciously control the use of non-verbal ways of communication.

1.1 RELATIONSHIPS

The way people use space communicates something about their relationships.
Use the sketches as a basis for discussion.

Is either person at an advantage (i.e. in a dominant position)?

What difference does *distance* make?

What difference does *height* make?

What difference does *the table* make?

You are a secretary organising a board meeting, or a hostess arranging an important dinner. Arrange the seating round the table to suit each occasion.

DISCUSSION

Use the diagrams of people round a table to answer these questions:

Which are the dominant positions? Which will make one of the people feel inferior?

If you were told to "pull up a chair and join in", where would you sit in each case?

ACTIVITY

Use tables and chairs to demonstrate.

3

1.2 OBJECTS

Objects can create interesting and satisfying shapes in a particular space (or place), as well as give information.

The photographs show rooms in which the furniture is arranged to tell you something of the function of the room.

How much can you tell about each room from its furniture and the way it is arranged?

What can you deduce about the people who use these rooms?

The arrangement of chairs and tables in your room at school says "classroom".

DISCUSSION

How does the layout of these class-rooms reflect what can or can not happen in lessons?

ACTIVITY

Using the tables and chairs in your classroom, or sketches to represent them, make your room say:

* a coffee lounge
* a conference room
* a block of home units

1.3 PEOPLE IN SPACES

Suggest a title for each of the photographs.
The photographs give some information about what the people are doing and about their relationships with one another.

DISCUSSION

Discuss how space is used to give this information. Consider particularly the position of people in relation to each other and to objects.

What effect does *purpose* have on the arrangement of people and space?
What effect does status or rank have?
What effect can cultural tradition have?

Discuss what you think is a comfortable space to have between you and someone else in an everyday social situation. How do you feel if a stranger invades this space? (i.e. your territory).

ACTIVITY

Work in pairs. One of you speaks volubly of the events of the day. The other has never met you before, tries to explain this and backs away. The speaker follows. What happens to the distance between you?
Find another partner.

* Fan meets pop star or sporting celebrity.
* Subject meets royal personage.

Observe changes in body shape relating to differences in status as each speaks to the other.

Practical work on the use of space.

Set up a scene (i.e. arrange the space) in your classroom to give the following information:

a. A group of friends is playing cards. A new arrival would like to participate but the group does not want an outsider to join in the game.

b. A committee of three board members of equal status is interviewing applicants for a scholarship.

c. A doctor's receptionist is talking on the phone. Three patients arrive. As there are no empty chairs, they wait near the desk. The talk continues. Show that:
    * nobody in the room knows anybody else
    * nobody wants to be seen as listening to the phone conversation

d. *Scene I*: The office of a government minister who likes to impress government officials with the dignity and importance of his work. The minister is at work on his papers when a junior employee comes in with a request.

    Scene II: The room where the same government minister receives members of his electorate. To them he likes to appear one of the people—homely and approachable. Show the minister in his room as a voter comes in.

We can use space to demonstrate the meaning of a word by making that word concrete.

The dictionary defines *spiral* as *winding continually about and constantly receding from a centre.*

Illustrate this by drawing a spiral or by producing an example such as a watch spring. Now use people to demonstrate the spiral shape.

What is a *labyrinth*?
Use people to show what a labyrinth looks like. Keep working until everyone agrees that it is right.

2 MOVEMENT OR STILLNESS

2.1 WAYS OF BEING STILL WHAT DOES STILLNESS TELL?

Phrases like *jumping for joy* or *frozen with fear* show the way we use words to link movement (or lack of movement) with feeling. We express our feelings in the way we move, and our stillness may communicate what we are feeling more surely than words.

In the way we use language, we associate certain ways of moving with different animals. So a mouse might scurry, a swallow glide and a duck waddle.

a. Discuss the differences there might be in the quality of the stillness of a cat in these situations. How does the situation affect muscle tension and relaxation?
    * You are a cat, motionless, watching a bird on the grass. The unsuspecting bird moves closer
    * You are a cat, motionless, deep in sleep
    * You are a cat, motionless, too hot to move
    * You are a cat, motionless, out of reach of a threatening dog

b. This is an exercise to make you aware of, and able to control, tension and relaxation in your own body.
    Lie on your back so you do not intrude on anyone else's space.
    Clench your feet. Release.
    Clench your calf muscles. Release.
    Clench your thigh muscles. Release.
    Tighten your stomach. Release.
    Tighten your chest muscles. Release.
    Clench your fists. Release.
    Tighten your forearms. Release.
    Tighten your neck and shoulders. Release.

Grit your teeth and scrunch up your face. Release.
Now tense your whole body from toe to head. Release.
Slowly melt into the floor.

c. Using a and b together:
    Imagine you are at home, sitting in a chair, waiting for someone who is late.
    You might be feeling—
    * bored—there's nothing to do
    * tired—you didn't get much sleep
    * impatient—you want to get going
    * angry—you said you wouldn't bother waiting for this person again
    * relaxed—you appreciate some time to yourself
    * sick—you've had a headache since lunch
    * worried—you might have mistaken the time
    * sleepy—you're enjoying a fantasy

Select one of these or another of your own choice, and let the others tell you what feeling your *waiting* communicates.

2.2 **WAYS OF MOVING**

a. Suppose you had to become one of the following: a bear; a mouse; a wagtail; an eagle; a spider; a dog (choose your breed if you like).

How would your build affect the kinds of movements you make? the speed of the movements?

Work in small groups, helping each other to perfect the movements of the identity you have chosen. Use the whole body.

b. Our occupation, as well as our physique, influences the way we stand and sit and move.

Imagine yourself as one of the following:
* a model on the cat walk
* a policeman on the beat
* a robot
* a soldier on the parade ground
* an old person going for a walk

Show how you would stand, sit, move and pause. Consider the way your whole body moves, as well as parts like arms, legs and head.

c. Suppose you were teaching the meaning of some adverbs to someone who knew little English. How would you show the differences between:—
* Walking *aggressively*
* Walking *stealthily*
* Walking *drunkenly*

Demonstrate one of these walks, or another of your choice. Let the group label it with the suitable adverb, so you can assess how accurate your explanation has been.

d. A series of connected movements can tell a story. This extract from *Move* by Bronwen Nicholls is given to you to mime. Try miming it at normal speed first, with someone reading the text aloud. Concentrate on remembering the sequence of actions. When you can remember this, try the sequence in fast motion (as in silent films), then in slow motion (as in a sport replay). Do not omit any detail and keep your movements accurate.

It is morning. The alarm rings. You lie in bed pulling the blankets over your head to cut out the sound. But the sunshine pours through the window. It's too hot under the bedclothes. Out you get; stretch, yawn, reach for a dressing gown, pull it on, wander down the hall, open the front door, pick up the newspaper and bottle of milk from the step, go back inside and close the door with your foot.

2.3 MOVEMENT INDICATES INTENTION

What Am I Doing? The aim of the following exercise is to recall an action and reproduce it accurately.

Use movement without any props to communicate the following:—

* * I am chopping wood
* * I am threading a needle
* * I am cleaning my teeth

Do these actions at a normal speed. Then try each of them in slow motion so you can focus on each step. Ask yourself, for example, what else is involved in chopping wood besides raising the axe. Teach someone how to chop wood or thread a needle. Where would you begin? Make this the starting point for your individual activity.

What am I about to do? If someone climbed over the railing on the roof of a tall building, we might infer that the intention was to suicide.
What other reasons might there be? What would lead us to believe that it was a suicide attempt rather than something else?

Work in pairs. Use a movement to indicate your intention. Your partner reacts accordingly.

* * I intend to slap you
* * I intend to punch you
* * I intend to throw a ball to you
* * I intend to tell you off
* * I intend to kick you
* * I intend to embrace you
* * I intend to snub you

Study the photographs and decide what seems to be the intention of each person:
Work in threes. Two of you become the two persons in one of the pictures, taking up their exact positions. The third person checks this.
Now show the next movements of each of the two persons in turn, so that the intention, or any change of intention, becomes clear.

2.4 MOVEMENT SHOWS OUR FEELINGS

We may stamp our feet because we are in a rage, or because we are cold. It is hard to interpret the meaning of a movement unless we know the context in which it occurs, i.e. who does the movement, where it happens and why.

Work on the following exercises by concentrating on the action. Think of what you are doing and why you are doing it, and the feeling will show in your work.

A

You are feeling guilty because you promised to be home by midnight and you are an hour late. Your parents have gone to bed, but they are probably awake, waiting for you. You try to move from the front door to your bedroom without disturbing anyone.

Before you start this sequence of movements, picture your walk.

* Is it dark?
* What obstacles will you meet?
* How will you deal with each?
* If there is a light, where is it? Will you use it?
* What will tell you, as you move, if your progress is successful?
* When will you be able to relax your tension?

Now do the sequence. Did it work? If not, try again.

B

You are angry because you cannot persuade your parents to let you join a week-end holiday camp that everybody else is going to. You work off the anger as you hang out the washing.

Begin by picking up a peg in one hand and a piece of washing in the other. Peg it to the line, using as much energy as you can. Keep your feet firmly on the ground.

Now work in pairs. One bends down to pick up the peg and the washing. The other takes it and hangs it on the line. Increase the speed and force of your movements, creating a rhythm as you work.

C

You have an interview with a prospective employer. You desperately need this casual job.

Open the door. Enter. Shut the door. Walk across the room. Sit down. In this sequence of movements, show:

a. You are confident you will do well in the interview;

b. You are anxious about the interview because it is important;

c. You are apathetic because, although you need the money, you feel this is not much of a job.

d. You are aggressive because you think the interviewer could not possibly be on your side.

As you work on your movements, think about what makes us label one entry as confident and another as aggressive. Can you seem confident if you are feeling anxious?

D

Putting movement, purpose and feeling together.

Do the following actions, supplying details about your purpose and your feelings as indicated in the columns. Remember that, although each of you will do the exercise in an individual way, you are working to communicate (i.e. to make recognisable in your way) three things.
The scene is 5 o'clock in the street on a working day in the city.

ACTION	PURPOSE	FEELING
Office worker glances at watch, begins to run	?	?
A busker packs up	?	?
A young person walks up and down	?	?
An old person walks up and down	?	?
Three people stroll by	?	?

2.5 MOVEMENT EVOKES ATMOSPHERE

The slow, rhythmical walk of the pall-bearers at a state funeral helps to create the solemn atmosphere. Pall-bearers who ran, as you might envisage happening in a Monty Python show, could look funny.

Work on stillness and slow movements to convey the atmosphere of the following scene.

You have finished Christmas dinner on a very hot day. You are sitting outside in the shade of a tree waiting for the faintest breeze to relieve the heat.

It is 3 o'clock and, as the temperature is still rising, you drip with perspiration. You are so languid you can almost tolerate the small black flies.

What created the heaviness in your scene? the heat? the sense of fullness? the lack of energy?

2.6 TIMING

Timing a movement is an important part of the communication of its meaning.

A

Show the difference in meaning between these sentences in which the words are identical.
a. The Principal says, *Come here.* You come immediately.
b. The Principal says, *Come here.* Five seconds pass before you move.
What happens during the pause? Try different ideas.

B

The following movement exercises are designed to help you concentrate on timing your movements.

Firstly, work on the following gestures with your arms and legs, and involve the rest of your body: pushing, pulling, twisting, circling, wringing, rolling, flicking, dabbing, gliding, thrusting.

a. Now in groups of 8-10, make a washing machine. Some of the people in your group will form the shape of the washing machine. Some will be the clothes, water and detergent bubbles. Show what happens when the washing machine starts. Let it run at different speeds. Work on:—

* contrasting moments of comparative stillness and energetic tumbling and vibrating.

* contrasting levels of movement—e.g. some up, some down.

* contrasting direction of movement—e.g. forward and backward.

14

b. When you are satisfied with your interpretation of a washing machine, work out your own design for a machine that has a specific function. The machine can be realistic, e.g. a machine in a milk factory or it can be as imaginative as you can make it, so long as you demonstrate how this machine works, and what its use is. Concentrate on synchronising the timing of each part of the machine.

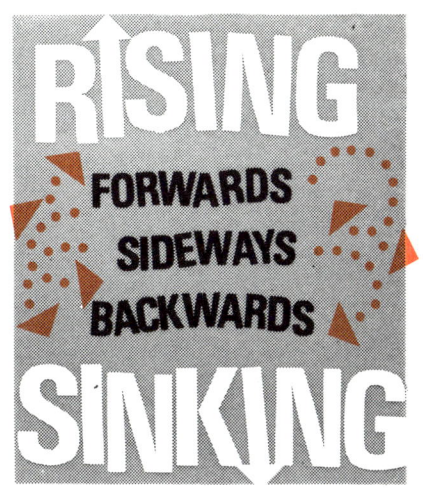

c. Simultaneous movement.

Work with a partner who will be your mirror. The mirror will reflect your actions. As in a mirror, there should be no time delay between action and reflection.

Work to the following rules:

* Face your partner who is an arm's length away

* Work in slow motion

* Use hands and arms only

* Look at your partner's forehead

It may take some time for you to get the actions and reflections identical. Change roles when you are making progress.

When you know your concentration is good, extend the rules, e.g. increase the speed; use your legs; move on different levels.

3 BODY STANCE AND GESTURE

3.1 COMMUNICATING MESSAGES

Using and responding to body language is something we learn without thinking about it. How do you interpret the following?

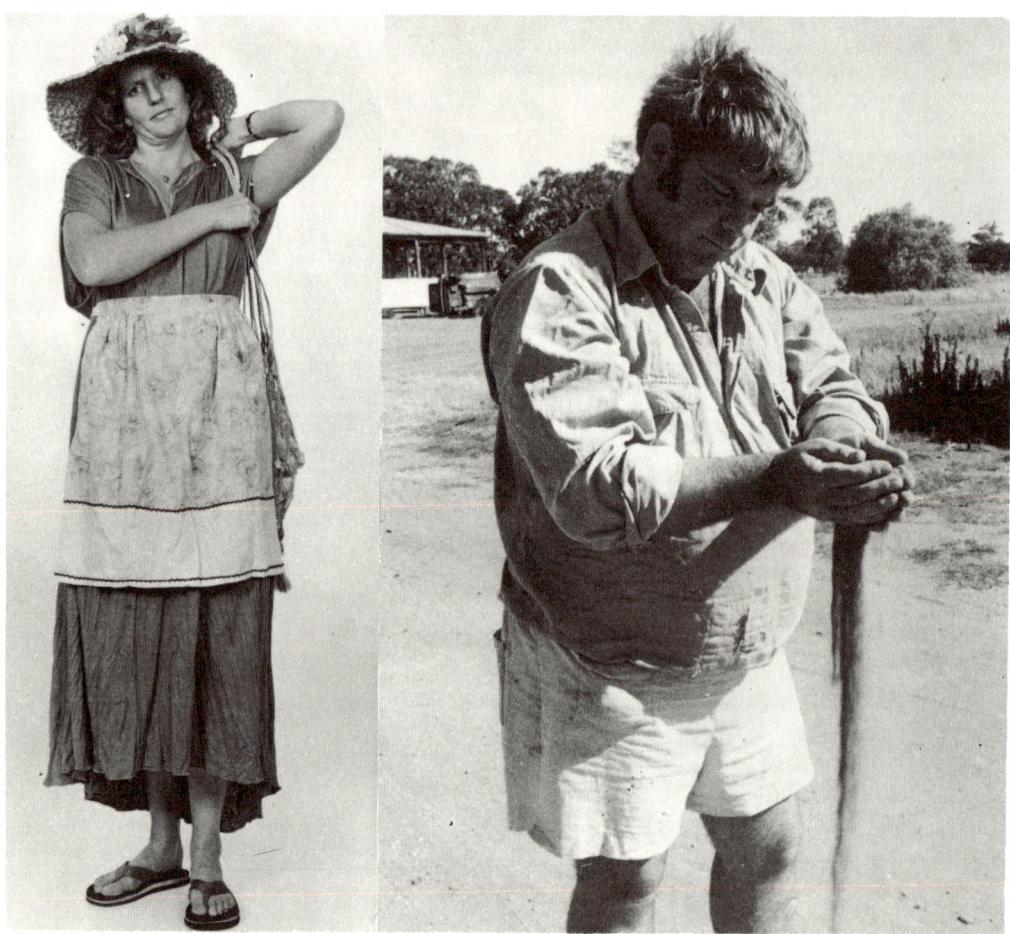

Use body language to say the following:
* Come here
* Wait there
* No
* I don't know
* Don't hit me
* Leave me alone

Suppose you are teaching in a school where none of the children speak English. Show them these words and phrases:
baby, bird, bread and butter, dog.

3.2 SHOWING FEELINGS

Body language (our gestures, facial expressions and posture) communicates our feelings to others. You may, for example, feel sure that somebody either likes or dislikes you. You sense when to approach your parents with a request, and when to leave it, by reading the signs.

Observing body language so we can recall, select and use it appropriately, is as important in real life as in drama. It might help if you close your eyes during the next exercise.

a. Think of someone you know well outside the classroom. See that person in your mind in a particular mood that might be typical. Concentrate on the picture, and slowly make yourself to be a replica of it.

Hold the position as you open your eyes. Focus on two other *replicas*. When you relax, tell the others your interpretation of their *pictures*.

b. It is easy to use stereotyped gestures (cliches) to communicate feeling, e.g. clasping the hands to indicate concern.

See how many cliches you can perform, while the others interpret. Now take the gesture of a *clenched fist*. How many things can you *say* with a *clenched fist*?

c. Even small changes in the way we use our hands can make a difference to what we communicate. Make the following gestures, and discuss the difference in the effect of each of the meanings each gesture might have:

* Clenched fists—forearm raised
* Clenched fists—hands near chest
* Clenched fists—hands by side
* Hand out, palm and arm fully extended
* Hand out, palm down and arm fully extended
* Hands near chest, the fingers clawed

d. Working without words and using as little movement as you can, let your body 'say' the following:—

* I am tired (so I'm going to sleep)
* I am tired (so leave me alone)
* I am tired (but I must finish)
* I am tired (and pleasantly relaxed)
* I am tired (and bored to death)

Choose one to work on, and let the others in the group tell you which one they see.

What precise differences do you notice in the way the body expresses different kinds of tiredness?

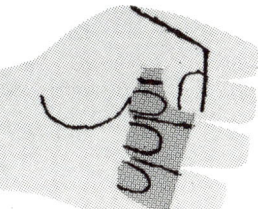

3.3 PRACTICAL EXERCISES

The exercises below give practice in using body language.

a. In pairs select one of the photographs to work on. Discuss what you think the subjects in the photograph are doing, thinking and feeling.

Write the dialogue between the persons in the photograph. Read it with the appropriate gestures. Try it several times, eliminating any gesture you think is unnecessary. Now eliminate the words.

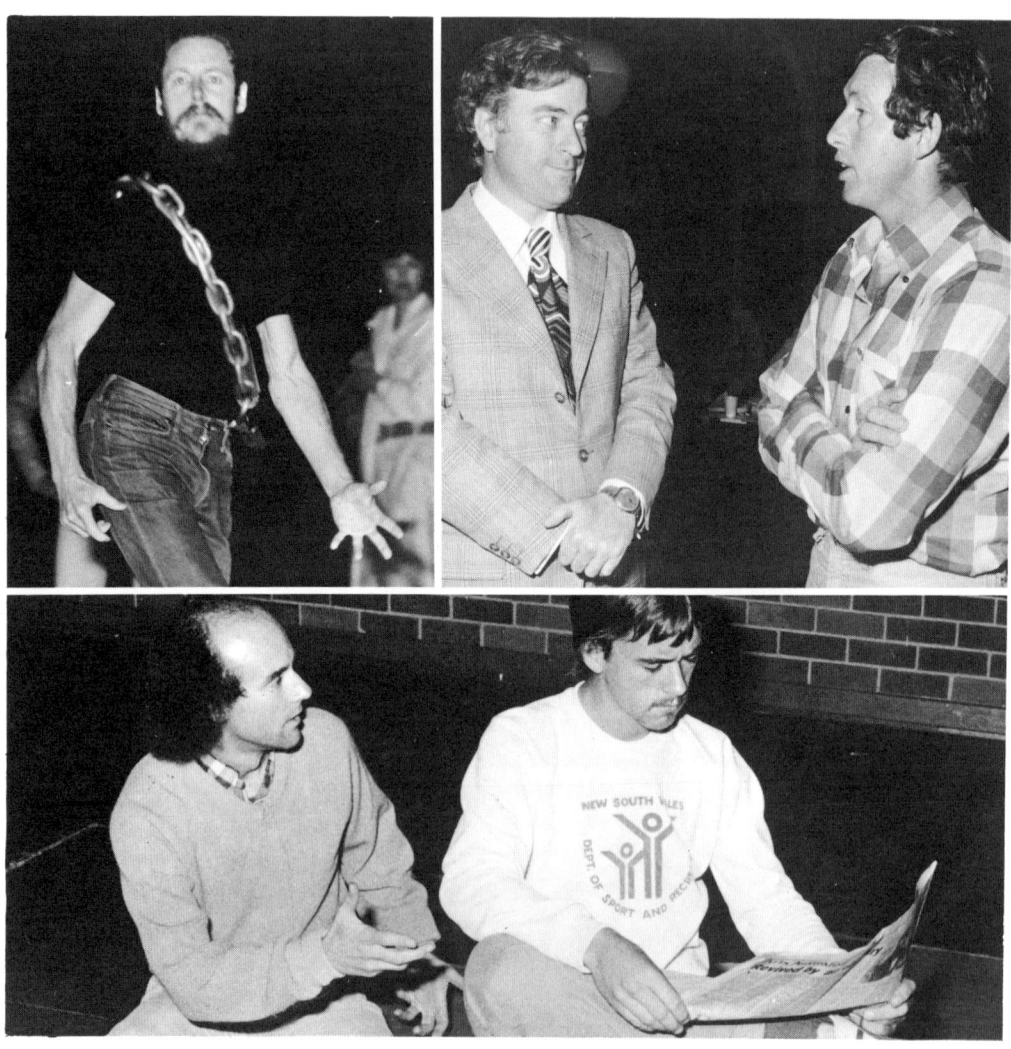

Show your work to the group. Did you find the minimum body language to communicate what the person in the photograph said?

b. Work with someone else for this exercise: S and C. S is a sculptor and C is a piece of clay. The sculptor is going to make from his clay a sculpture entitled *The Thinker*, *The Athlete*, *The Dancer*, *The Boxer*, (or some title of your choice). Decide together what your sculpture will be. Then C becomes clay and S creates the chosen sculpture.

Make sure you follow the rules. What, for example, can you do, or not do with clay? Don't forget the statue's facial expression!

Now reverse your roles, so S becomes clay and C the sculptor.

c. You are a tourist in a foreign country. You do not speak the language and you must find a bank immediately. You approach a policeman who must understand your request before directing you.

Now it's the policeman's turn to direct you on a very complicated route.

Remember—no words! You cannot get a satisfactory response unless you communicate your request precisely.

Now reverse the roles. It is the policeman's turn to be the tourist. This time, do not discuss what your need is beforehand. The tourist decides this before approaching the policeman.

d. The purpose of the last exercise in this section is to focus your attention on matching body language with words. If, for example, you say *I'm pleased to meet you*, accompany the words with a frown and stand with shoulders bunched and arms folded, then the person you speak to may not even hear the words.

Work in pairs to make up a simple advertisement in which one person is selling a product. The two of you then become the one person who is presenting the advertisement: A is the head, body and voice, B is the hands. You will need to stand or sit close, one behind the other. A's hands are folded behind, and B's hands and arms emerge as if they belonged to A. Work to synchronise the voice, facial expression and gestures.

4 CLOTHING AND ACCESSORIES

The clothing we wear may say something about our work, our interests, our personality, our social or financial status, or the way we would like people to see us.

4.1 CLOTHING GIVES INFORMATION

What can you tell about the people in the photographs from their clothing? Is more than one interpretation possible?

One of the photographs shows a person in uniform. What is the purpose of a school uniform? What effect might changing the colour or the style have on the uniform? . . . on people who wear it? . . . on people who see it?

Sketch something, in colour, you would choose to wear to school.

Use the photographs as a basis for discussing the proverb *Fine feathers make fine birds*.

Look at the photograph. See how much information you can get about the people (their jobs, etc.) from what they are wearing.

4.2 THE DRAMA WARDROBE

In drama, we consciously select costumes to project an image that people will recognise, or to reflect something of the character of the wearer. Colour and style (or line) are important aspects of costuming.

a. How would you dress someone to be instantly recognisable as:

* a businessman
* a coal miner
* a farmer
* a rock star
* a bride

Put your ideas into practice by choosing an identity for yourself and bringing to class what you need to make yourself recognisable as this identity. Restrict yourself to one item if possible (e.g. a hat, a piece of make-up, a curtain used in a particular way). You might like to create a comic effect by altering an expected style of dress.

b. You are dressing the characters in a play, and have been told that the colour each character wears must reflect character. What colours would you choose for:

* a flamboyant character
* a detached (cool) character
* a jealous character
* an innocent character
* an evil character

Make your own sketches. Use colour to create a colour scheme for the dress of one of the characters above or one of your own choice. Use at least one contrasting colour, for no character consists of a single trait.

Put your designs where they can be seen, and look at them from two points of view.

What quality of character does the use of colour suggest?

How pleasing is the way colour is contrasted and balanced?

4.3 ACCESSORIES

A uniform may identify the occupation and status of a person. A badge may tell you something about a person's interests or beliefs. A prop such as a white stick or a cigarette holder may help you get a picture of someone.

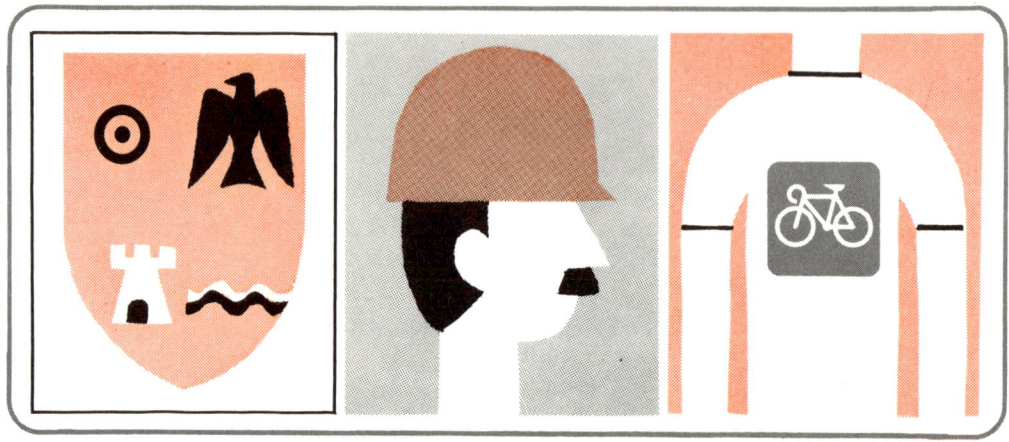

a. Decide on an identity for your group (conservationists? surfies? who?). On a sheet of paper (a continuous roll of newsprint is excellent) large enough for each group member to work on, design a badge that communicates the identity of your group (who you are, what you stand for). Use colour as part of your design.

b. Suppose you are a small business of three designing advertisements for T-shirts. Make a design, when you have decided:—

* the name of the product
* the age market you aim at

The T-shirt is white. Show your design (including words) in the colours you choose.

Badges and advertisements are part of our way of life. How much does a label (e.g. a badge, a T-shirt advertisement) reveal about the person wearing it? about the society in which the person lives? How much does the label conceal?

c. Cartoonists may use a prop like a pipe or a feature like a prominent chin to identify a public character. Bring to class a cartoon from a recent paper. Identify the person and the method of identification.

Work in pairs using no more than one prop to establish what is required in these situations. The props must come from the classroom or be made from what is in the room.

* One of you is a housewife opening the door to a salesperson
* One of you is a doctor examining an elderly patient
* One is a teenager talking to a parent
* One is a passenger and one is a bus conductor

As appearance alone does not make a salesperson or a doctor, work in pairs to establish your identity in a convincing way.

* Show where you are
* Do something to make clear what is happening
* Create minimum dialogue to accompany the action

d. It is often not so much the prop itself but the way it is used that is important. If you push a piece of wood into someone's back and say 'get moving', the person may not stop to ask if you have a real gun.
The following exercises are designed to help you focus on ways of using props and on thinking imaginatively (improvising).

* One person selects an object, e.g. a blackboard duster, and demonstrates its conventional use. The next person takes the duster and uses it as if it were something else—an ice-cream, a mouth organ, and so on, until everyone has had a turn.
* Extend your skill by repeating the last exercise in mime. The second person cannot take the object until the group recognises what it is from the way the first person is using it. The mime continues until each person has demonstrated the use of an object.

e. If you have a prop, use it. The prop should be related to what you do or are. If, for example, you want to show you are tense, you might carry a bag which you constantly open and close.
Select a prop (e.g. a feather duster) and use it to show one of the following aspects of character:
* I am disdainful
* I am flirtatious
* I have power
Now select any four props and put them on the table. e.g. an umbrella, a cigarette lighter, a brief case, and a towel. Each of the props belongs to an imaginary character.

In groups of four, make up a story involving the four characters and their props. Your story should make clear how the four characters are connected, and what relevance the four props have in the plot.
Show what happens in your story to the other groups.

5 SOUND OR SILENCE

5.1 SOUND—MUSIC

So far we have concentrated on visual communication. We now focus on sound. We hear many different kinds of sound in the course of a day. Music, words, laughter, and noises associated with machinery or animals, are part of life.

ACTIVITY

Lie on your back with your eyes closed. As before, clench and release your muscles from toe to head. Stay quite still for several minutes.

As the room grows quiet, make a mental note of every sound you hear.

At the end of the exercise compare notes in class discussion.

Was there any change in the kinds of sounds you heard?

Where did the sounds come from?

How was your sense of time affected?

DISCUSSION

It would be difficult to survive in an environment where there was no sound, yet sound affects people in different ways.

Discuss how different people may be affected by music. How important are other factors, such as beat and volume, besides the kind of music in determining enjoyment? Give examples to back up what you say.

What difference, if any, is there between music and noise? . . . between words and noise? . . . between noises and noise?

What relationship, if any, can you see between music, words and noise?

26

5.2 MUSIC

Employers would not have considered introducing music into a factory in the nineteenth century. Now piped music is often taken for granted.

What do you think would be the effect on your work and that of others if music were played during the school day?

What subjects would best benefit from background music?

If you support the idea of music during lessons, name specific pieces you would play. Play some of these to test the reaction of the group.

5.3 MUSIC AND DRAMA

In this section we mention three of many ways to use music in drama.

A

Music may be used to mark a special occasion. *The Star Spangled Banner* might be played at an American Independence Day parade.

Suggest suitable music for:—
* the arrival of a royal personage at a banquet
* a burial
* a Labour Day march

B

Music may be used to create atmosphere.

Discuss the music you think would best suit the following occasions. Name specific pieces and play them. Discuss in your group the atmosphere each piece creates?

* A dinner date with someone you are trying to impress
* A dinner for your parents' twenty-fifth wedding anniversary
* A party with your friends
* An evening alone—you want to think
* A fête where everyone is being encouraged to spend money
* A New Year's Eve celebration in a city square

C

Music is a way of linking parts of a story together. The following is a sequence of events which may be linked by music and emphasised by music (atmospheric music).

The owner locks up his restaurant . . .

Walks to his parked car . . .

Checks nobody is watching . . .

Unlocks the door . . .

Sits behind the wheel . . .

Feels a gun in his back . . .

Hears a voice saying . . .

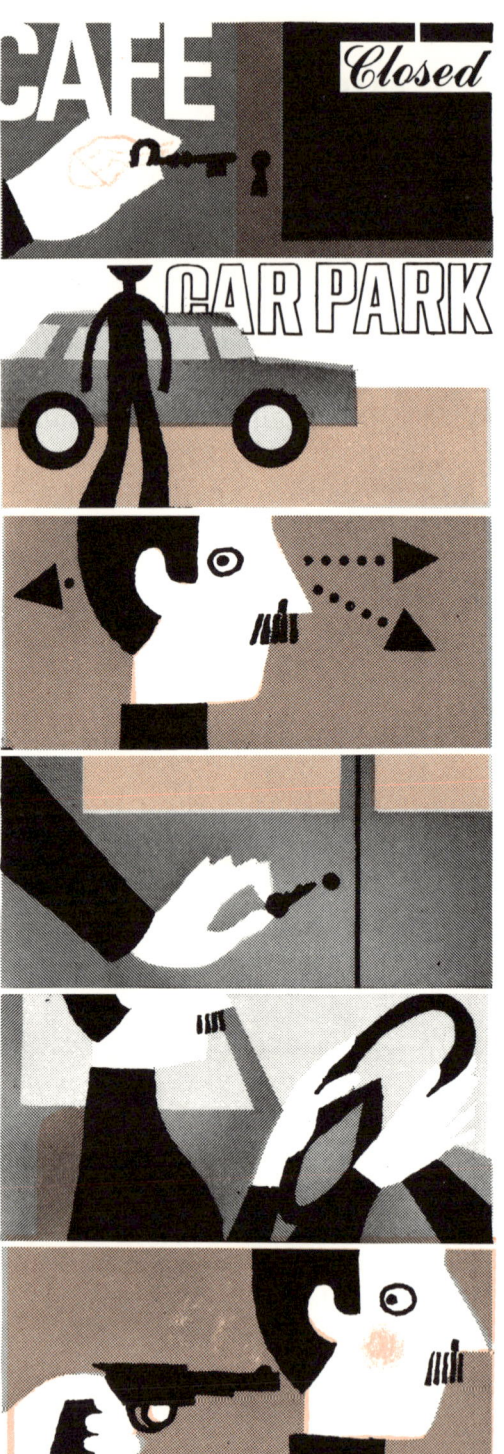

At what point would you introduce the music? Where would you stop it?

In what part of the sequence should the music be loudest? When should the tempo alter?

How should it alter? Quicker or slower?

Have someone do the actions while you experiment with the music.

Now create your own story and the music to accompany it. Make a sequence of events, or several short episodes and use music as a way of bridging the time differences.

Make a 'sound track' on a tape recorder. Use bongo drums, tambours, tambourines, triangles, cymbals, xylophones, woodblocks, maracas, etc. Try making your own instruments, or borrow some from the music department. Make sounds with your voices.

5.4 MUSIC AND WORDS

I Saw a Man is from Kenneth Cook's play *Stockade*, the basis of which is the Eureka Stockade, a significant and bloody confrontation between miners and authority in the development of Australia.

a. The simplicity and the repetition in this song make it a good example of music used to convey something important.

Experiment with different ways of making an impact with your presentation of I Saw a Man. *These questions may give you some ideas:—*

How could you use a drum beat to emphasise repetition in the verses?

How could you emphasise the conversational nature of the song?

How could you use speaking voices to replace the singing voice or voices (if no piano or taped accompaniment is available)?

In what way could you emphasise the growing bitterness of the words? (Consider the preceding stage direction).

I SAW A MAN

I saw a man go marching off to war, to war,
I saw a man go marching off to war.
I said to him 'Why do you go
with the flags above and your drums below?'
And he replied: 'I'm sure I don't know what for...'

I saw a man go kill a man in a war, a war,
I saw a man go kill a man in war.
I said to him 'Why should you kill
that other man. Did he do you ill?'
And he replied: 'I'm sure I don't know what for...'

I saw a man lie wounded in a war, a war,
I saw a man lie wounded in a war.
I said to him: 'Why are you blind,
and why have you left your leg behind?'
And he replied: 'I'm sure I don't know what for...'

I saw a man a'dying in a war, a war,
I saw a man a'dying in a war.
I said to him: 'Why should you die
and in the ground forever lie?'
And he replied: 'I'm sure I don't know what for...'

b. Watch an advertisement on TV when music is used, and answer the following questions:—
   * When does the music play? (Before, after, or during speech?)
   * What effect does the particular music have? How noticeable is the music?
   * What changes (e.g. in volume) are there in the music? How do you explain these changes?

In a group, work on creating a short advertisement for an imaginary product. Your purpose is to use suitable music in your work (a tape, a guitar, voices, a drum, etc.). Include a 'jingle'.

5.5 SOUND AND ITS MEANING

Once we have heard the sound of a car accident, or a jet taking off, we can attach meaning to the sound. Sometimes we hear sounds we cannot identify and sometimes we are so used to hearing sounds, we are not aware of them.

ACTIVITY

Try the following group exercise to sharpen your ability to interpret the sounds you hear and give you practice in connecting sounds to make meaning.

On a cassette, record three different sounds. Each recording should be of sufficient length for listeners to have a chance to identify it. The sounds may be of little significance in themselves—like the sound of a biro marking paper, or pins dropping into a tray. Do not record easily recognisable sounds like the barking of a dog.

Give your tape to another group to play.

Groups work separately—
* To identify the sounds.
* To make up a story that involves the three sounds.
* To show the class what happens in the story. Find a way of making with your voices the three sound effects as each occurs in your story.

DISCUSSION

Discuss your interpretations of the sounds.

How did you make your interpretations?

In the previous exercise, you were asked to give meaning to isolated sounds. Context generally helps us to determine the meaning of a sound.

Demonstrate the significance of the ticking clock in the following situations. Set up each scene.

* You glance at the clock. You have ten minutes to complete the examination.
* The prisoner is in his cell, awaiting execution at dawn. The only sound he can hear in the dark is the ticking of the clock.

5.6 SPEECH SOUNDS AND MEANING

In speech we signal meaning not only by our words, but by the way we say them.

A TONE

Tone of voice is particularly important in establishing meaning. It tells us what the feeling of the speaker is, and we can recognise and respond to this without understanding a word.

Say the sentence *I'm hungry*

> having returned home after a hard day's work
>
> as a starving beggar

How do you recognise the difference?

Create three or four lines of speech in which the tone is appropriate to the following situations. Remember, there are many different ways of saying these things, depending on who you are, where you are, your relationship to the other person, your purpose and your attitude to the subject. Decide whether you are to be forceful, overbearing, polite, diffident, confident, etc.

Work in pairs. Try out your speech on your partner, who will react to your tone. Then reverse roles.

* Tell someone that smoking is not permitted in the workshop.
* Tell someone who has assumed that you both vote for the same political party that you are fundamentally opposed to that party.
* Answer the phone and tell the caller that your boss is out. Offer your help.
* Tell the waiter or waitress that the coffee is not acceptable. You want another cup.

B EMPHASIS

Emphasis on certain words in speech clarifies meaning

a. *Lorraine might be staying with us for Christmas.* Say this to suggest:
   * Lorraine (not Jim) will be staying with us
   * It is doubtful that Lorraine will stay
   * Lorraine will stay with us (instead of with her family)
   * Lorraine normally does not stay
   * Lorraine will stay with us for Christmas (not some other time)

   What conveys to you the meaning in each case?

b. Read the following short pieces aloud. Discuss where you will put emphasis. Give reasons for your decisions.

EPIGRAM by John Dryden

HERE LIES MY WIFE
HERE LET HER LIE
NOW SHE'S AT REST
AND SO AM I!

From **THE MERCHANT OF VENICE**
by William Shakespeare

Shylock, a Jewish moneylender, hates Antonio, and tells us why. Try to capture the tone of this aside.

SHYLOCK [*aside*].
How like a fawning publican he looks!
I hate him for he is a Christian!
But more, for that, in low simplicity,
He lends out money gratis, and brings down
The rate of usance here with us in Venice.
If I can catch him once upon the hip,
I will feed fat the ancient grudge I bear him.
He hates our sacred nation; and he rails,
Even there where merchants most do congregate,
On me, my bargains, and my well-won thrift,
Which he calls interest. Cursed be my tribe,
If I forgive him!

From **UNDER MILK WOOD** by Dylan Thomas

In speaking these lines, the first voice is describing the people in a small town in Wales. Work on contrasting softness and loudness, as well as on emphasis.

FIRST VOICE. (*Very softly.*) It is Spring, moonless night in the small town, starless and bible-back, courters'-and-rabbits' wood limping invisible down to the sloeblack, slow, black, crowblack, fishing boat-bobbing sea. The houses are blind as moles (though moles see fine to-night in the snouting, velvet dingles) or blind as Captain Cat there in the muffled middle by the pump and the town clock, the shops in mourning, the Welfare Hall in widows' weeds. And all the people in the lulled and dumbfound town are sleeping now.

Hush, the babies are sleeping, the farmers, the fishers, the tradesmen and pensioners, cobbler, school-teacher, postman and publican, the undertaker and the fancy woman, drunkard, dressmaker, preacher, policeman, the webfoot cocklewomen and the tidy wives. Young girls lie bedded soft or glide in their dreams, with rings and trousseaux, bridesmaided by glow-worms down the aisles of the organ-playing wood. The boys are dreaming wicked or of the bucking ranches of the night and the jollyrodgered sea. . . . You can hear the dew falling, and the hushed town breathing.

From THE IMPORTANCE OF BEING EARNEST
by Oscar Wilde.

Wilde is poking fun at the snobbish English upper classes. Use emphasis as a way of underlining the patterns of each character's speech, (e.g. the repetitions), as well as the sense of the speech.

ALGERNON.   . . . Now, my dear boy, if we want to get a good table at Willis's, we really must go and dress. Do you know it is nearly seven?

JACK.   Oh! it is always nearly seven.

ALGERNON.   Well, I'm hungry.

JACK.   I never knew you when you weren't.

ALGERNON.   What shall we do after dinner? Go to a theatre?

JACK.   Oh, no! I loathe listening.

ALGERNON.   Well, let's go to the Club.

JACK.   Oh, no! I hate talking.

ALGERNON.   Well, we might trot around to the Empire at ten?

JACK.   Oh, no! I can't bear looking at things. It is so silly.

ALGERNON.   Well, what shall we do?

JACK.   Nothing!

ALGERNON.   It is awfully hard work doing nothing. However, I don't mind hard work where there is no definite object of any kind.

C CHANGE IN PITCH

Altering the pitch (making the voice higher or lower) or volume (making the voice louder or softer) affects the meaning of speech.

The punctuation marks help you to adjust the pitch of your voice in these two sentences. Read them aloud.

* You're not going with me!
* You're not going with me?

What is the difference in meaning?

ACTIVITY

To help you control the pitch and volume of your voice, practise breathing in this way . . .
Stretch your diaphragm muscle to fill your lungs with air. Slowly release it so that the air flows smoothly out of your slightly open lips. Breathe in again and recite the numbers up to ten clearly, in one breath. Breathe normally again. Take in another long breath and try to count up to fifteen. Now up to twenty if you can. (Remember that each of us has a different lung capacity, so don't worry if you can't get that far. Get as far as you comfortably can.) Try the same exercise using the days of the week or the months of the year, using varying volume and pitch.

Go back to the extracts from *The Merchant of Venice* and *Under Milk Wood*. How important is pitch or variety in pitch in bringing these extracts to life?

D PROJECTION

Sometimes it is difficult to hear all the words of a speaker, because the voice of the speaker is not directed towards you.

ACTIVITY

To check your voice projection, prepare to tell a joke or make a short speech. Focus on some person or spot towards the back of the classroom as you tell your joke or make your speech. You may whisper so long as your words are clearly heard.

FOCUS ▷

E CHANGE OF PACE

Changes of pace (from fast to slow) influence the communication of meaning.

a. The house is on fire. Phone the fire brigade superintendent and tell him how to get there.

You are going for a country walk. Ask a farmer how to get to the nearest shop.

During your explanation, your partner is not allowed to ask questions, and must repeat your explanation when you have finished.

Discuss how suitable was the pace of your speech. Was it geared to your task?

b. In this extract from *Romeo and Juliet* by William Shakespeare, Juliet, alone, realises she must now drink the potion which will make her seem dead until Romeo returns to rescue her. As you read each phrase, use changes in the pace, pitch and volume to mirror Juliet's questioning and doubts.

Contrast, for example, the speed with which you say line 7 and line 8. Where is the moment of decision for Juliet? How will you indicate this?

JULIET.   Farewell! God knows when we shall meet again.
I have a faint cold fear thrills through my veins,
That almost freezes up the heat of life:
I'll call them back again to comfort me:
Nurse? What should she do here?
My dismal scene I needs must act alone.
Come, vial.
What if this mixture do not work at all?
Shall I be married then tomorrow morning?
No, no; this shall forbid it. Lie thou there.
        (*Laying down a dagger*)
What if it be a poison, which the friar
Subtly hath minister'd to have me dead,
Lest in this marriage he should be dishonor'd,
Because he married me before to Romeo?
I fear it is: and yet, methinks, it should not,
For he hath still been tried a holy man.
How, if, when I am laid into the tomb,
I wake before the time that Romeo
Come to redeem me? there's a fearful point!
Shall I not then be stifled in the vault,
To whose foul mouth no healthsome air breathes in,
And there die strangled ere my Romeo comes?

F PUTTING IT TOGETHER

Read the following extracts, trying to bring them to life by concentrating on tone and the variety of pace, pitch and volume that will reflect the meaning of words.

··

From PRIDE AND PREJUDICE by Jane Austen

This is a conversation between Mr and Mrs Bennet. The writer's comments give information about the characters that will help you to decide your tone of voice and the pace of the dialogue.

"My daughters have none of them much to recommend them", replied Mr Bennet, "they are all silly and ignorant, like other girls, but Lizzy has something more of quickness than her sisters".

"Mr Bennet, how can you abuse your own children in such a way! You take delight in vexing me. You have no compassion on my poor nerves."

"You mistake me, my dear. I have a high respect for your nerves. They are my old friends. I have heard you mention them with consideration these twenty years at least."

"Ah! you do not know what I suffer."

"But I hope you will get over it, and live to see many young men of four thousand a year come into the neighbourhood."

"It will be no use to us, if twenty such should come, since you will not visit them."

"Depend upon it, my dear, that when there are twenty, I will visit them all."

Mr Bennet was so odd a mixture of quick parts, sarcastic humour, reserve, and caprice, that the experience of three-and-twenty years had been insufficient to make his wife understand his character. Her mind was less difficult to develop. She was a woman of mean understanding, little information, and uncertain temper. When she was discontented, she fancied herself nervous. The business of her life was to get her daughters married; its solace was visiting and news.

From **THE WAY OF THE WORLD** by William Congreve

Lady Wishfort, as her name implies, wishes to marry Sir Rowland, and is preparing for his visit. She is trying to decide how she can make the best impression on Sir Rowland.

Work on varying the pace of this speech and on using pauses to mirror her thinking—her decision and indecision.

Lady Wish. Well, and how shall I receive him? in what figure shall I give his heart the first impression? there is a great deal in the first impression. Shall I sit?—no, I won't sit—I'll walk—ay, I'll walk from the door upon his entrance; and then turn full upon him—no, that will be too sudden. I'll lie—ay, I'll lie down—I'll receive him in my little dressing-room, there's a couch—yes, yes, I'll give the first impression on a couch.—I won't be neither, but loll and lean upon one elbow: with one foot a little dangling off, jogging in a thoughtful way—yes—and then as soon as he appears, start, ay, start and be surprised, and rise to meet him in a pretty disorder—yes—O, nothing is more alluring than a levee from a couch, in some confusion:—it shows the foot to advantage, and furnishes with blushes, and recomposing airs beyond comparison. Hark! there's a coach.

From THE KILLERS by Ernest Hemingway

Al and Max are sitting at the counter in Henry's lunchroom. They are dressed like twins in overcoats too tight for them. They sit leaning forward, elbows on the counter.

THE door of Henry's lunchroom opened and two men came in. They sat down at the counter.

"What's yours?" George asked them.

"I don't know," one of the men said. "What do you want to eat, Al?"

"I don't know," said Al. "I don't know what I want to eat."

Outside it was getting dark. The street light came on outside the window. The two men at the counter read the menu. From the other end of the counter Nick Adams watched them. He had been talking to George when they came in.

"I'll have a roast pork tenderloin with apple sauce and mashed potatoes," the first man said.

"It isn't ready yet."

"What the hell do you put it on the card for?"

"That's the dinner," George explained. "You can get that at six o'clock."

George looked at the clock on the wall behind the counter.

"It's five o'clock."

"The clock says twenty minutes past five," the second man said.

"It's twenty minutes fast."

"Oh, to hell with the clock," the first man said. "What have you got to eat?"

"I can give you any kind of sandwiches," George said. "You can have ham and eggs, bacon and eggs, liver and bacon, or a steak."

"Give me chicken croquettes with green peas and cream sauce and mashed potatoes."

"That's the dinner."

"Everything we want's the dinner, eh? That's the way you work it."

"I can give you ham and eggs, bacon and eggs, liver—"

"I'll take ham and eggs," the man called Al said. He wore a derby hat and a black overcoat buttoned across the chest. His face was small and white and he had tight lips. He wore a silk muffler and gloves.

"Give me bacon and eggs," said the other man. He was about the same size as Al. Their faces were different, but they were dressed like twins. Both wore overcoats too tight for them. They sat leaning forward, their elbows on the counter.

"Got anything to drink?" Al asked.

"Silver beer, bevo, ginger ale," George said.

"I mean you got anything to *drink*?"

"Just those I said."

"This is a hot town," said the other. "What do they call it?"

"Summit."

"Ever hear of it?" Al asked his friend.

"No," said the friend.

"What do you do here nights?" Al asked.

"They eat the dinner," his friend said. "They all come here and eat the big dinner."

"That's right," George said.

"So you think that's right?" Al asked George.

"Sure."

"You're a pretty bright boy, aren't you?"

"Sure," said George.

"Well, you're not," said the other little man. "Is he, Al?"

"He's dumb," said Al. He turned to Nick. "What's your name?"

"Adams."

"Another bright boy," Al said. "Ain't he a bright boy, Max?"

"The town's full of bright boys," Max said.

George put the two platters, one of ham and eggs, the other of bacon and eggs, on the counter. He set down two side dishes of fried potatoes and closed the wicket into the kitchen.

"Which is yours?" he asked Al.

"Don't you remember?"

"Ham and eggs."

"Just a bright boy," Max said. He leaned forward and took the ham and eggs. Both men ate with their gloves on. George watched them eat.

"What are *you* looking at?" Max looked at George.

"Nothing."

"The hell you were. You were looking at me."

"Maybe the boy meant it for a joke, Max," Al said.

George laughed.

"*You* don't have to laugh," Max said to him. "*You* don't have to laugh at all, see?"

"All right," said George.

"So he thinks it's all right." Max turned to Al. "He thinks it's all right. That's a good one."

"Oh, he's a thinker," Al said. They went on eating.

"What's the bright boy's name down the counter?" Al asked Max.

"Hey, bright boy," Max said to Nick. "You go around on the other side of the counter with your boy friend."

"What's the idea?" Nick asked.

"There isn't any idea."

"You better go around, bright boy," Al said. Nick went around behind the counter.

"What's the idea?" George asked.

"None of your damn business," Al said. "Who's out in the kitchen?"

"The nigger."

"What do you mean the nigger?"

"The nigger that cooks."

"Tell him to come in."

"What's the idea?"

"Tell him to come in."

"Where do you think you are?"

"We know damn well where we are," the man called Max said, "Do we look silly?"

"You talk silly," Al said to him. "What the hell do you argue with this kid for? Listen," he said to George, "tell the nigger to come out here."

"What are you going to do to him?"

"Nothing. Use your head, bright boy. What would we do to a nigger?"

George opened the slit that opened back into the kitchen. "Sam," he called. "Come in here a minute."

The door to the kitchen opened and the nigger came in. "What was it?" he asked. The two men at the counter took a look at him.

"All right, nigger. You stand right there," Al said.

Sam, the nigger, standing in his apron, looked at the two men sitting at the counter. "Yes, sir," he said. Al got down from his stool.

"I'm going back to the kitchen with the nigger and bright boy," he said. "Go on back to the kitchen, nigger. You go with him, bright boy." The little man walked after Nick and Sam, the cook, back into the kitchen. The door shut after them. The man called Max sat at the counter opposite George. He didn't look at George but looked in the mirror that ran along back of the counter. Henry's had been made over from a saloon into a lunch counter.

"Well, bright boy," Max said, looking into the mirror, "why don't you say something?"

"What's it all about?"

"Hey, Al," Max called, "bright boy wants to know what it's all about."

"Why don't you tell him?" Al's voice came from the kitchen.

"What do you think it's all about?"

"I don't know."

"What do you think?"

Max looked into the mirror all the time he was talking.

"I wouldn't say."

"Hey, Al, bright boy says he wouldn't say what he thinks it's all about."

"I can hear you, all right," Al said from the kitchen. He had propped open the slit that dishes passed through into the kitchen with a catsup bottle. "Listen, bright boy," he said from the kitchen to George. "Stand a little further along the bar. You move a little to the left, Max." He was like a photographer arranging for a group picture.

"Talk to me, bright boy," Max said. "What do you think's going to happen?"

Read the extract aloud as dialogue. Then set up the scene, and move as the words suggest.

What tone of voice do you think Al and Max use? How can you make us hear the differences between Al and Max, and George and Mick? At what pace should the scene move?

5.7 SILENCE AND MEANING

a. Silence can speak louder than words. Work in twos.
  * A is accusing. B silently admits guilt.
  * A expresses an opinion. B silently signifies agreement.
  * A is assertive. B silently protests.

b. John has been questioned by the Principal about an incident involving several people, including his brother. John refuses to say anything.
How might these people interpret his refusal? . . .
  * His best friend
  * His girl friend
  * His teacher
  * The Principal of his school
  * His parents

c. Silence may be short or long. It may be punctuated by words in different ways.

What are you doing?
    (no reply)
I said 'what are you doing?'.
Try reading these lines as:
  * parent to child
  * child to parent
  * wife to husband
  * nurse to patient who is deaf
  * teacher to pupil
  * friend to friend
How long is the pause after the first question in each case?
What happens during the pause (the silence)?
How does the pause affect the repetition?

There are different ways of saying *yes*. These depend upon how you feel about the question and the questioner. The time you take to answer the question reveals something of your feeling.

Answer this question to express the meanings given:

Question: Do you believe in God?

Answer: Yes.
  * I am a strong convinced believer.
  * I have thought much about it.
  * Obviously you want me to say *yes*, but the answer is *no*.
  * It's not a simple question, but the answer is nearer to *yes* than *no*.
  * It's not a simple question, but the answer has to be *yes*.
  * I don't want you to ask me any more questions.

A DRAMATIC PAUSES

In this extract, some of the pauses are indicated in the script. As you read the extract, taking the parts of the old woman and the old man, decide how long these, and any other pauses, must be.

What happens when there is no talking? What do the silences communicate? Work on the scene and perform it. Experiment with the pace of the dialogue.

From **CAN'T YOU HEAR ME TALKING TO YOU**
by Nora Dugon

OLD MAN.   Never satisfied, are you? Nothing but whinging. Everything's my fault.

OLD WOMAN.   Who's going on now? (*Long pause.*) And close that window. You know that draught's bad for my arthritis.

OLD MAN.   (*rising, throwing down paper*) Oh! you and your arthritis! (*Slams window shut, sits down, angrily folds paper.*)

OLD WOMAN.   (*after a long pause*) Anything in the paper?

OLD MAN.   Nothing.

OLD WOMAN.   Never anything in it. Can't see why you buy it.

OLD MAN.   How about a cup of tea?

OLD WOMAN.   I'm knitting. (*Pause.*) Anyway, *if* he's coming we can wait and have one then.

OLD MAN.   Who's coming? (*Turning page of paper.*) You mean Peter?

OLD WOMAN.   Who else? We've only got one son, haven't we?

OLD MAN.   Well, he only said he might come. He only said maybe.

OLD WOMAN.   Still . . . we can wait.

(OLD MAN *reading, dozes off.*

OLD WOMAN *stops knitting, stares straight ahead.*)

The following exercise is designed to help you focus on *timing*. (When, for instance, you must begin speaking, or when you must pause.)

When we are faced with a difficult or awkward situation, for example, telling someone we have dinted his car, we may cover up by making small talk or laughing nervously. Or we may be hesitant, wondering how to begin.

The following situations might be described as *difficult*. In groups of eight, discuss how you would go about each task, and how you would react to different approaches.

Work in pairs to prepare one of the situations to show to the group. Concentrate on timing. When do you broach the matter? When do you react? How long are intervening pauses? What do the pauses represent? What *happens* during pauses? . . . movement? . . . gesture? . . . stillness?

* The Prime Minister has to sack a senior colleague.
* The treasurer of a society has to tell the president that he has embezzled money over a long period.
* A soldier, decorated for bravery, has to tell the commanding officer that he hid during the battle.
* The conductor of a choir has to ask a life-long member to resign.

5.8 SEEING OR NOT SEEING

We have examined the use of visual communication and communication through sound and silence in drama. Now we briefly examine the use of *seeing through our ears* in drama.

Sometimes what we see has less effect on us than what we do not or cannot see. Using our imagination, we can build something, whether it exists or not, so that in our minds it is larger, more terrifying, more beautiful or more real than it would be if we could actually see it.

Whether to make something visible or not is an important decision in drama. We are now going to use some of the playwrights' techniques, like eye-witness accounts and observation of people's reactions, to make something *real*, although it is not visible.

A newspaper editor decides to manufacture a story that a spaceship has landed in the Blue Mountains. He tells his staff that the story must be so convincing that the public will want to read about it—ensuring publication of thousands more copies of the paper. The editor instructs his reporters to:—

* Hypothesise—think up some convincing possible reasons for the spaceship's arrival.
* Interview—people who can be persuaded to believe they have seen something to support the presence of the spaceship.
* Deduce—information about the activities of the spaceship by inventing the behaviour of people nearest the location of the spaceship.
* Research—previous reports of alleged spacecraft in the area.

* Corroborate—the possibility of the presence of a spacecraft by academic or other authorities.
* Visualise—the spacecraft for readers by making an artist's impression.
* Sketch—everyday objects found in the area. Infer their use in this context.

Form 7 groups of reporters to work on one of the editor's instructions.

When you have completed the task, present your reports to the editor for publication.

Do a 'mockup' of the front page of your newspaper, focussing attention on your reports using Headlines, Pictures and Layout.

From Act 1, Scene 2 of **MACBETH**
by William Shakespeare

Shakespeare could have written a battle into the script, and a director would stage it. However, we do not see the battle. We see a badly wounded sergeant who gives first-hand information about the battle. Through his eyes, we get a strong impression of Macbeth's ferocity as a soldier before we meet him, as well as an account of the battle.

When you have read the sergeant's speech, list the information given about the battle and Macbeth. In groups, organise the information as a news report. Choose one of you to be newsreader and present the report.

As you read the sergeant's speech aloud, we must see someone who is badly wounded but who still has sufficient strength to fulfil his function of giving information before he collapses.

* Although the sergeant is wounded, this is of less interest than the information he brings. How can the information be emphasised?
* The sergeant's strength is limited. How will this affect, e.g. the pace at which he speaks?
* How does the news affect Duncan and the others? Show the reactions.

Read the script carefully, answering the following questions to help you bring it to life.

* What information does Duncan give about the appearance and bearing of the sergeant? Translate this information into body language.
* Who might support the sergeant? How might the sergeant be supported to emphasise his pain? ... his fatigue? ... his position before the king?

The sergeant created the battle for us to see by his words, his appearance and his actions. In the same way, we can create special effects. Suppose, e.g. you want to show that you and your companion are lost in the blinding sand of the desert.

In pairs, work out the minimum:—

* action you might do
* words you might say to establish this convincingly

Play the scene.

SCENE 2

A camp near Forres.

Alarum within. Enter DUNCAN, MALCOLM, DONALBAIN, LENNOX, *with* ATTENDANTS, *meeting a bleeding* SERGEANT.

DUNCAN.   What bloody man is that? He can report,
              As seemeth by his plight, of the revolt
              The newest state.

MALCOLM.   This is the sergeant
              Who, like a good and hardy soldier, fought
              'Gainst my captivity.—Hail, brave friend!
              Say to the king thy knowledge of the broil
              As thou didst leave it.

SERGEANT.   Doubtful it stood;
              As two spent swimmers, that do cling together
              And choke their art. The merciless Macdonwald—
              Worthy to be a rebel, for, to that,
              The multiplying villainies of nature
              Do swarm upon him—from the western isles
              Of kerns and gallowglasses is supplied;
              And fortune, on his damned quarrel smiling,
              Show'd like a rebel's whore: but all's too weak,
              For brave Macbeth,—well he deserves that name,—
              Disdaining fortune, with his brandish'd steel,
              Which smok'd with bloody execution,
              Like valour's minion,
              Carv'd out his passage till he fac'd the slave;
              Which ne'er shook hands, nor bade farewell to him
              Till he unseam'd him from the nave to th' chops,
              And fix'd his head upon our battlements.

DUNCAN.   O valiant cousin! worthy gentleman!

SERGEANT.   As whence the sun 'gins his reflection
              Shipwracking storms and direful thunders break
              So from that spring, whence comfort seem'd to come,
              Discomfort swells. Mark, king of Scotland, mark:
              No sooner justice had, with valour arm'd,
              Compell'd these skipping kerns to trust their heels,
              But the Norweyan lord, surveying vantage,
              With furbish'd arms and new supplies of men,
              Began a fresh assault.

DUNCAN. Dismay'd not this
Our captains, Macbeth and Banquo?

SERGEANT. Yes;
As sparrows eagles, or the hare the lion.
If I say sooth, I must report they were
As cannons overcharg'd with double cracks;
So they
Doubly redoubled strokes upon the toe:
Except they meant to bathe in reeking wounds,
Or memorize another Golgotha,
I cannot tell:—
But I am faint, my gashes cry for help.

DUNCAN. So well thy words become thee as thy wounds;
They smack of honour both.—Go get him surgeons.
[*Exit* SERGEANT, attended.]

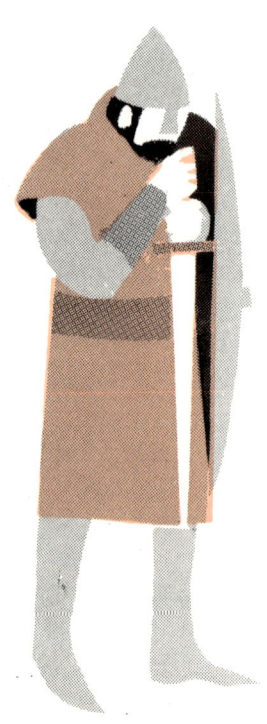

BRINGING
A SCRIPT
TO LIFE

To give you practice in using the non-verbal elements in drama, short scripts follow.

You may choose to work as a class, polishing your work, or you may like to work in groups, showing the others your interpretation.

The questions and suggested activities accompanying the extracts may help you bring the scenes to life.

6.1 From **NORM AND AHMED** by Alexander Buzo

Much of the strength of the opening of *Norm and Ahmed* by the Australian writer, Alexander Buzo, depends on the economical use of language and non-verbal elements such as pause. How, for example, does Buzo use a cigarette to build tension in the stage directions at the beginning? ... in the first exchange between Norm and Ahmed? How does he use contrasting movements, including stillness (pause) to build tension?

CHARACTERS

NORM, a strongly-built, middle-aged man
AHMED, a slim young Pakistani student

SCENE

A footpath on a Sydney street under some scaffolding in front of a construction site. A white fence at the back, about five feet high, and then a wire-mesh fence rising above it. The scaffolding is supported by two posts at the front, which are joined by a handrail. There is a bus stop on one side and a garbage tin on the other.
Midnight on a summer night.

Lights up on NORM, *who is leaning against the fence. He wears an open necked white shirt and grey trousers. A clock strikes twelve.* NORM *moves around restlessly, looking up and down the street. He takes out a cigarette packet, looks in it, then screws it up and flings it on the ground angrily. He brings out a fresh packet, rips off the Cellophane with his teeth and takes out a cigarette, which he lights with a lighter. He moves around a bit more and then leans on the fence again. He waits. Then he starts moving around some more, and suddenly straightens up, looking to his left. He puts his cigarette out and takes another from the packet, putting it in his mouth unlit. He leans casually against the fence. The sound of footsteps is heard and* AHMED *appears, wearing a Nehru-style suit and carrying a briefcase. He walks past* NORM.

NORM: Excuse me, mate.

(AHMED *stops and looks at* NORM. *Pause.*)

Got a light?

AHMED: Yes, certainly.
(*He offers a box of matches.*)

NORM: Thanks.
(*He keeps the matches after he has lit up.*)

I was dying for a smoke. Lucky you turned up.
Nothing open at this hour.

AHMED: No, it's nearly midnight.

(*Pause.* AHMED *has been waiting for* NORM *to return his matches, but now he starts to edge away wearily.*)

NORM: Wait a minute, mate.

AHMED: Yes?
(*Pause.*)

NORM: You forgot your matches.

(*He holds them out.*)

AHMED: (*taking them warily*) Thank you.
(*He edges away.*)

In the scene you have just worked on, Norm is on the offensive and Ahmed is on the defensive. Perform the scene again, improvising an ending in which Norm continues on the offensive. Now show what happens if the scene ends with Ahmed taking the offensive.

Discuss how believable your endings are, following the build-up of tension.

6.2 ACT WITHOUT WORDS by Samuel Beckett

Read the short mime *Act Without Words* and get some idea of the sequence of action.

Use a narrator at first to discipline the pace at which you do the mimes. Then try the following improvisation to sharpen your sense of timing.

* You share a flat with someone. You get up at the same time in the morning to go to work. One of you is by nature slow and lethargic. The other is quick and nervous. Work out a routine that enables you both to catch the 8.15 bus.

> **NOTE**
>
> This mime should be played on a low and narrow platform at back of stage, violently lit in its entire length, the rest of the stage being in darkness. Frieze effect.
>
> A is slow, awkward (gags dressing and undressing), absent. B brisk, rapid, precise. The two actions therefore, though B has more to do than A, should have approximately the same duration.

ARGUMENT

Beside each other on ground, two yards from right wing, two sacks, A's and B's, A's being to right (as seen from auditorium) of B's, i.e. nearer right wing. On ground beside sack B a little pile of clothes (C) neatly folded (coat and trousers surmounted by boots and hat).

Enter goad right, strictly horizontal. The point stops a foot short of sack A. Pause. The point draws back, pauses, darts forward into sack, withdraws, recoils to a foot short of sack. Pause. The sack does not move. The point draws back again, a little further than before, pauses, darts forward again into sack, withdraws, recoils to a foot short of sack. Pause. The sack moves. Exit goad.

A, wearing shirt, crawls out of sack, halts, broods, prays, broods, gets to his feet, broods, takes a little bottle of pills from his shirt pocket, broods, swallows a pill, puts bottle back, broods, goes to clothes, broods, puts on clothes, broods, takes a large partly eaten carrot from coat pocket, bites off a piece, chews an instant, spits it out with disgust, puts carrot back, broods, picks up two sacks, carries then bowed and staggering on his back half way to left wing, sets them down, broods, takes off clothes (except shirt), lets them fall in an untidy heap, broods, takes another pill, broods, kneels, prays, crawls into sack and lies still, sack A being now to left of sack B.

Pause.

Enter goad right on wheeled support (one wheel). The point stops a foot short of sack B. Pause. The point draws back, pauses, darts forward into sack, withdraws, recoils to a foot short of sack. Pause. The sack moves. Exit goad.

B, wearing shirt, crawls out of sack, gets to his feet, takes from shirt pocket and consults a large watch, puts watch back, does exercises, consults watch, takes a tooth brush from shirt pocket and brushes teeth vigorously, puts brush back, rubs scalp vigorously, takes a comb from shirt pocket and combs hair, puts comb back, consults watch, goes to clothes, puts them on, consults watch, takes a brush from coat pocket and brushes clothes vigorously, brushes hair vigorously, puts brush back, takes a little mirror from coat pocket and inspects appearance, puts mirror back, takes carrot from coat pocket, bites off a piece, chews and swallows with appetite, puts carrot back, consults watch, takes a map from coat pocket and consults it, puts map back, consults watch, takes a compass from coat pocket and consults it, puts compass back, consults watch, picks up two sacks and carries them bowed and staggering on his back to two yards short of left wing, sets them down, consults watch, takes off clothes (except shirt), folds them in a neat pile, consults watch, does exercises, consults watch, rubs scalp, combs hair, brushes teeth, consults

and winds watch, crawls into sack and lies still, sack B being now to left of sack A as originally.

Pause.

Enter goad right on wheeled support (two wheels). The point stops a foot short of sack A. Pause. The point draws back, pauses, darts forward into sack, withdraws, recoils to a foot short of sack. Pause. The sack does not move. The point draws back again, a little further than before, pauses, darts forward again into sack, withdraws, recoils to a foot short of sack. Pause. The sack moves.

Exit goad.

A crawls out of sack, halts, broods, prays.

Curtain

Return to the script to work on the positioning of characters. Mark in the original position of A and B. Trace the action in the script on the plan, using arrows. Go through the movements to see if they work, and make necessary alterations.

As you begin to work through the script again, discuss how A and B are different. How are they the same?

Work particularly on movement, pace and body stance to bring the mime to life.

53

6.3 From **WEST SIDE STORY by** Laurents and Sondheim

Two groups: one group is talking angrily amongst themselves; the other group muttering fearfully. Within each group move continuously so that you keep changing the person to whom you are speaking.

On a given signal (e.g. a tambour beat) the angry group focuses together on the fearful group and freezes. The other group focuses back. Your frozen position should indicate your emotion. Now talk amongst yourselves again, this time each group reversing the emotion. On the signal focus again and freeze in a shape.

Now read the script and divide into two groups, one Sharks and one Jets.

Set up a group picture in which you communicate the tension between Sharks and Jets.

a. In this tableau, Jets position themselves first to 'possess' the area. Use different levels, variety in body posture. The Jets have names. Think up names for the Sharks.
    What do these names suggest about their characteristic gestures and movements?

b. Sharks enter gradually, each Shark marking a Jet. Take up a body shape which suggests conflict with your opponent.
    Does the total arrangement suggest tension between the groups?

c. The tableau comes to life.
    In pairs, in the tableau positions, devise two gestures each that say *Shark* or *Jet*. Make your movements and gestures aggressive.
    Experiment with the pace of your movements, the contrast between levels and the direction in which you move, and the kind of movements and gestures you choose, e.g. *shark*—glide and dive around jet at varying speeds; *jet*—flick and thrust at shark from high position.

Start again. The Jets are now in possession of the area.
The timing of the arrival of the first of the sharks is important. How does he enter? Work on crisp movements to contrast with the over-elaborate apologies. Other Sharks enter in twos and threes. Read the script carefully. When will you use occasional words—("I am so sorry")?

The fight is half-mimed, half-danced. The work on stage fights that follows may give you ideas to adapt to the interaction here.

The police enter when the fight is at its height. The fight stops, and Jets and Sharks greet the police with charm and innocence.

To make the reaction of the gang credible, how will you present the police? Show the contrast before and after the arrival of the police, and discuss what non-verbal means you are using.

5.00 p.m. The street.

A suggestion of city streets and alleyways; a brick wall.

The opening is musical: half-danced, half-mimed, with occasional phrases of dialogue. It is primarily a condensation of the growing rivalry between two teen-age gangs, the Jets and the Sharks, each of which has its own prideful uniform. The boys—sideburned, long-haired—are vital, restless, sardonic; the Sharks are Puerto Ricans, the Jets an anthology of what is called American.

The action begins with the Jets in possession of the area: owning, enjoying, loving their 'home'. Their leader is Riff: glowing, driving, intelligent, slightly whacky. His lieutenant is Diesel: big, slow, steady, nice. The youngest member of the gang is Baby John: awed at everything, including that he is a Jet, trying to act the big man. His buddy is A-rab: an explosive little ferret who enjoys everything and understands the seriousness of nothing. The most aggressive is Action: a cat-like ball of fury. We will get to know these boys better later, as well as Snowboy: a bespectacled self-styled expert.

The first interruption of the Jets' sunny mood is the sharply punctuated entrance of the leader of the Sharks, Bernardo: handsome, proud, fluid, a chip on his sardonic shoulder. The Jets, by far in the majority, flick him off. He returns with other Sharks: they, too, are flicked off. But the numerical supremacy, the strength of the Jets, is gradually being threatened. The beginnings of warfare are mild at first: a boy being tripped up, or being sandbagged with a flour sack or even being spit on—all with over-elaborate apologies.

Finally, Arab comes across the suddenly deserted area, pretending to be an aeroplane. There is no sound as he zooms along in fancied flight. Then over the wall drops Bernardo. Another Shark, another and another appear, blocking Arab's panicky efforts to escape. They close in, grab him, pummel him, as a Shark on top of the wall is stationed as look-out. Finally, Bernardo bends over Arab and makes a gesture (piercing his ear); the lookout whistles; Jets tear on, Sharks tear on, and a free-for-all breaks out. Riff goes at once to Arab, like a protective father. The fight is stopped by a police whistle, louder and louder, and the arrival of a big goon-like cop, Krupke, and a plain-clothes man, Schrank. Schrank is strong, always in command; he has a charming, pleasant manner, which he often employs to cover his venom and his fear.

PLANNING A FIGHT SCENE

To help you plan the fight sequence work in pairs on several of the following fight techniques.

The Face Slap. Make sure your opponent is just beyond your reach. Swing a slap (forehand or backhand) and follow through. The better your opponent's reaction, the more realistic the Face Slap looks. Get someone else to clap their hands at the moment of 'impact' as an offstage sound effect.

The Upper Cut. Once again, make sure your opponent is just beyond your reach. Swing a punch and follow through. Your opponent reacts with a backwards jerk of the head on 'impact'.

The Stomach Punch. 'Pull' your punch a short distance from your opponent's stomach. (On your own, practise 'pulling' punches beforehand!) Your opponent's sudden body contraction could then be followed by an uppercut from either of you.

The Foot Stomp. 'Stomp' a couple of inches to one side of your opponent's foot. A quick lift of the 'injured' foot, a yell of pain and a few hops will make the reaction believable.

The Hair Pull. Place a closed, empty fist on your opponent's head. Your opponent grasps your wrist with both hands, firmly keeping your fist in position as you pull. Once again, a well acted reaction will make it seem as if you are pulling your opponent along by the hair.

The Nose Pull. Place two curved fingers on either side of your opponent's nose, taking care not to actually squeeze it. Again, your opponent grasps your wrist, firmly holding your fingers in position as you pull.

Falling in Stages. Sit on the ground and practise flopping loosely to either side. Kneel up, collapse the legs and flop. Crouch, sink to kneel, collapse the legs and flop. From a half-stand, sink to crouch, then to kneel, collapse the legs and flop. Practise this sequence, pausing for a moment at each stage. Remember, the more released the muscles, the less likely you are to hurt yourself when you land. Practise until these separate actions now have a smooth, continuous flow. When you feel really confident, stand up and fall to the floor!

Now very carefully make up a short fight sequence based on several of the above techniques. Rehearse the sequence in slow motion until each action/reaction flows smoothly into the next, with no pauses in between. When you are sure that neither of you is likely to get hurt, speed up the sequence each time you do it.

Use your rehearsed fight as part of the half-mimed, half-danced street fight in the previous 'West Side Story' sequence.

6.4 From **HAMLET** by William Shakespeare

In this short extract from the beginning of *Hamlet*, Shakespeare sets the time, and the dialogue gives information that helps us to feel and see the scene as the watch changes.

Prepare the scene, working on movement and gestures to show:
* The changing of the watch
* The cold
* The lateness of the hour

ACT I.   SCENE 1

Elsinore.   A platform before the castle.

FRANCISCO *at his post. Enter to him* BERNARDO.

BERNARDO.   Who's there?

FRANCISCO.   Nay, answer me: stand, and unfold yourself.

BERNARDO.   Long live the king!

FRANCISCO.   Bernardo?

BERNARDO.   He.

FRANCISCO.   You come most carefully upon your hour.

BERNARDO.   'Tis now struck twelve; get thee to bed, Francisco.

FRANCISCO.   For this relief much thanks: 'tis bitter cold, And I am sick at heart.

BERNARDO.   Have you had quiet guard?

FRANCISCO.   Not a mouse stirring.

BERNARDO.   Well, good night. If you do meet Horatio and Marcellus, The rivals of my watch, bid them make haste.

FRANCISCO.   I think I hear them.—Stand, ho! Who is there?

Enter HORATIO *and* MARCELLUS.

HORATIO.   Friends to this ground.

MARCELLUS.   And liegemen to the Dane.

FRANCISCO.   Give you good night.

MARCELLUS.   O, farewell, honest soldier: Who hath reliev'd you?

FRANCISCO.   Bernardo has my place. Give you good night. [*Exit*].

MARCELLUS.   Holla! Bernardo!

BERNARDO.   Say,—What, is Horatio there?

HORATIO.   A piece of him.

6.5 THE SEVEN DEADLY SINS from DR FAUSTUS
by Christopher Marlowe

Use what you have learnt to work out a way of presenting the *Seven Deadly Sins*. The questions alongside the text may guide your thinking.

When you have prepared the scene, find modern equivalents for each sin. How would each dress? On what occasion might these sins parade together? Who could be in control of the occasion? Who would be the audience of today?

How would you group Belzebub, Faustus, Lucifer and Mephostophilis?

BELZEBUB. Faustus, we are come from hell in person to show thee some pastime. Sit down and thou shalt behold the seven deadly sins appear to thee in their own proper shapes and likeness.

FAUSTUS. That sight will be as pleasant to me as Paradise was to Adam the first day of his creation.

How would each sin enter? What kind of music would you use? ... electronic? ... live? ... percussive? ... taped?

How could you group the sins to best effect? At what point in the entertainment might you vary the picture?

LUCIFER. Talk not of Paradise or Creation, but mark this show. Talk of the devil and nothing else. Go, Mephostophilis, fetch them in.

Enter the SEVEN DEADLY SINS.

BELZEBUB. Now, Faustus, question them of their names and dispositions.

FAUSTUS. That shall I soon. What art thou, the first?

What tone of voice would Pride use?

What gesture could Pride make here?

How might you vary the pace in this speech? For what purpose?

PRIDE. I am Pride. I disdain to have any parents. I am like to Ovid's flea. I can creep into every corner of a wench. Sometimes like a periwig I sit upon her brow. Next, like a necklace I hang about her neck. Then, like a fan of feathers, I kiss her. And then turning myself to a wrought smock do what I list. But fie, what a smell is here! I'll not speak a word for a king's ransome, unless the ground be perfumed and covered with cloth of Arras.

FAUSTUS. Thou art a proud knave indeed. What art thou, the second?

What accessory might suggest Covetousness?

COVETOUSNESS. I am Covetousness. Begotten of an old churl in a leather bag. And might I now obtain my wish, this house, you and all, should turn to gold, that I might lock you safe into my chest. Oh, my sweet gold!

What colour might be suitable for Envy to wear?

FAUSTUS.　And what art thou, the third?

ENVY.　I am envy, begotten of a chimney-sweeper and an oyster-wife. I cannot read and therefore wish all books were burnt. I am lean with seeing others eat. Oh, that there would come a famine over all the world, that all might die, and I live alone, then thou should'st see how fat I'd be. But must thou sit and I stand? Come down, with a vengeance!

FAUSTUS.　Out, envious wretch. But what art thou, the fourth?

What kind of movement does Wrath make?
What make-up could help to suggest Wrath?

WRATH.　I am Wrath. I had neither father nor mother. I leapt out of a lion's mouth when I was scarce an hour old, and ever since have run up and down the world with this case of rapiers, wounding myself when I could get none to fight withal. I was born in hell, and look to it, for some of you shall be my father.

FAUSTUS.　And what art thou, the fifth?

What props might help to suggest Gluttony?

GLUTTONY.　I am Gluttony. My parents are all dead, and the devil a penny they have left me, but a small pension and that buys me thirty meals a day and ten bevers: a small trifle to suffice nature. I come of a royal pedigree; my father was a gammon of bacon and my mother was a hog's head of claret wine. My godfathers were these: Peter Pickle-herring and Martin Martlemas-beef. But my godmother, oh, she was an ancient gentlewoman, and well-beloved in every good town and city. Her name was Mistress Margery March-beer. Now, Faustus, thou hast heard all my progeny, wilt thou bid me to supper?

FAUSTUS.　No, I'll see thee hanged. Thou'wilt eat up all my victuals.

GLUTTONY.　Then the devil choke thee.

FAUSTUS.　Choke thyself, Glutton. What art thou, the sixth?

How can movement, posture and voice help to suggest Sloth?

SLOTH.　Hey ho, I am Sloth. I was begotten on a sunny bank where I have lain ever since, and you have done me great injury to bring me from thence. Let me be carried thither again by Gluttony and Lechery. I'll not speak another word for a king's ransom.

What does the word 'Minx' suggest about Lechery?
What action might suggest Lechery?

What do these lines tell the director about the sins?
... about Faustus' reaction?

FAUSTUS.   And what are you, Mistress Minx, the seventh and last?

LECHERY.   Who, I, sir? I am one that loves an inch of raw mutton better than an ell of fried stockfish, and the first letter of my name begins with Lechery.

FAUSTUS.   Away to hell! Away, on, piper!

Exeunt the SEVEN DEADLY SINS.

LUCIFER.   Now, Faustus, how dost thou like this?

FAUSTUS.   Oh, this feeds my soul.

LUCIFER.   Tut, Faustus, in hell is all manner of delight.

FAUSTUS.   Oh, might I see hell and return again safe, how happy were I then!

LUCIFER.   Faustus, thou shalt. At midnight I will send for thee. Meanwhile, peruse this book and view it throughly, and thou shalt turn thyself into what shape thou wilt.

FAUSTUS.   Thanks, mighty Lucifer. This will I keep as chary as my life.

LUCIFER.   Now, Faustus, farewell, and think on the devil.

FAUSTUS.   Farewell, great Lucifer. Come, Mephestophilis:

Exeunt omnes, several ways.

7 DEVELOPING SKILLS IN DRAMA

7.1 MOVEMENT WITH PURPOSE

In drama, as in life, we perform ordinary actions like walking, sitting and eating, and we communicate our reason for doing the action (our intention) by the way we do it. There are many reasons, for example, for reading a book. We may wish to relax, to study or to appear inconspicuous.

In this section we move from the recognition of the non-verbal elements of drama to the development of skills in selecting, using and interpreting material for drama.

Suppose you wish to demonstrate *sitting down to read a book for relaxation*. You might make your action credible by working out a series of small actions which help to say *relaxation*.

a. You are at home. You pick up your book which is lying open on the table.

b. As you walk towards your comfortable chair, you stop and take an apple from the bowl on the sideboard.

c. You take a bite of the fruit as you move to the chair.

d. You sit in the chair, getting yourself into a comfortable position. Are you far enough back in the chair? Is the light sufficient?

e. As you begin reading, you take another bite of the apple. You read the last line on the page and turn to the next.

When a number of you have demonstrated the action of reading a book for relaxation, choose another reason for reading. Work out a series of actions that will communicate your reason and demonstrate the action.

While each demonstration will be unique because each person performs actions in an individual way, there will be differences between the two ways of reading a book.

What makes the difference?

How is the difference communicated?

Read the following short scenes. Each involves the action of *walking to the door*. Picture each scene to yourself, and the series of movements that lead you to walk to the door. Use a few words if they help to make your action feel right in the situation.

* You have had a row with your parents. You tell them you are leaving home. You walk to the door, open it, walk out and slam it.

* You have shut yourself in your room because you want to be alone. You think everyone must have gone out because you can hear nothing. You walk to the door and listen.

* Devise your own short scene with a reason for *walking to the door*.

Work in pairs. A performs and B interprets the reason. Now change roles.

7.2 ACTION AND CHARACTER

The way a person performs an action may reflect something of the character of the doer. All chefs, for example, may go through the same process in making puff pastry, yet one chef may be relaxed in the way he throws in the flour, while another measures the flour with great care.

You are a nervous, inexperienced thief opening a window on the ground floor of a block of units.

What tools do you have?

How do you check you are not observed?

At what speed do you work?

Try the series of actions, beginning with your movement to the window. Now try the same sequence as:
* a confident, experienced thief
* an over-confident, inexperienced thief

Discuss the differences you observed in the way the three thieves moved and took precautions. How would each react if seen?

Repeat the sequences, adding your reaction on being discovered.

You are a taxidriver closing the door of your taxi—
* To test the lock you have just repaired
* To end an argument with someone on the footpath
* For some other reason

Work by yourself to decide what kind of person the taxidriver is, and what his attitude is to his job.

In groups, demonstrate your taxidriver shutting the door for a specific reason.

Others in the group will describe to you your character and your reason for shutting the door, so you can evaluate your communication.

7.3 ACTION AND REACTION

So far we have concentrated on doing actions alone. Often someone else is involved in what we are doing, so there is a process of action and reaction.

Work in pairs: A and B. Hold the *knife* firmly in your hand. Feel its weight. Indicate to your partner the length of your knife. Now face each other, knife point to knife point, and each take one long step back to allow movement. On a given sound (e.g. the beat of a drum), A lurches at B who reacts simultaneously to avoid the strike. Both fighters freeze in this position. On the next signal, B lunges and A reacts.

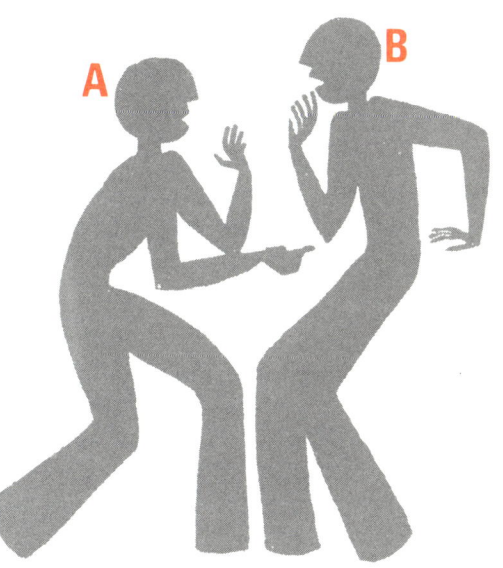

Experiment with lunges from different angles and levels. Preserve the two-knife distance between you so you do not *knife* the other.

Try the fight in slow motion, e.g. lunge and avoid to the count of 5, so you can work with accuracy, concentrating on simultaneous thrust and reaction.

Add this knife fight to your West Side Story sequence.

7.4 USING WORDS

So far we have been concentrating on action and reaction in movement. Now we use a similar technique with words.

A *The word association game.*

The first person says a word. The second responds with a word in some way associated with the first. And so on until everyone has had one or more turns.

e.g. milk - - - - cheese - - - - biscuit - - -

In the situation outlined below, the action of the sales promoter triggers a reaction from each shopper. The reaction is related to the shopper's character.

Decide who will play the parts (you can write in others) and set up the scene.

Storyline: You are employed to promote the sales of a well-known brand of soap by offering free cakes to shoppers in a shopping centre.

Offer the soap so the shopper cannot resist accepting it.

Each shopper will react by doing an action that says:

First shopper:	I am greedy for a free gift.
Second shopper:	I don't believe it.
Third shopper:	I couldn't care less about your free gift.
Fourth shopper:	I don't want to be approached in a public place.

Work on the movement in the scene until you are satisfied with the communication. Each shopper's reaction might influence the way the promoter offers the soap to the next person.

B *Action and reaction in conversation.*

Work in pairs to build a conversation in which one of you begins by saying: 'I shouldn't have got out of bed this morning'.

Describe a series of disasters. B reacts either sympathetically or unsympathetically. What effect does B's attitude have upon A's discourse? Now change roles.

As a group, discuss which responses helped to build conversation. Which hindered it?

Change pairs and use the same technique to build conversations beginning:
'Guess what happened today.'
'We need money soon.'

Try to build an amusing conversation, then a serious one, from each beginning.

Suppose you are a confident, helpful person. You see someone at a party who is too shy to join in. You decide to try to talk with the person.

Decide which of the two characters you want to play. Do not prepare any words or topics of conversation beforehand. Remember that the confident person's intention is to make the other person more comfortable, so it is important to listen to each response to see if you are progressing.

C Action and reaction to build a crowd scene.

a. Work in twos. Hold a short conversation, using 'phrases' made up of numbers, or days of the week, or months of the year. Listen carefully to your partner's inflexions and try to react to them with meaningful inflexions of your own, so that the conversation almost seems to make sense.

b. Change partners and try some more conversations in different moods: happy, sad, gossipy, angry, fearful, conspiratorial, etc.

c. Now move around, constantly changing partners, keeping all conversations in one particular mood.

d. Following an 'off-camera' visual hand signal (try not to make it obvious that you are looking out for it!), keep changing the volume of the crowd noise on a sliding scale from quiet to loud. At a given visual signal, everyone stops talking and you all focus in the same direction. Each time you do this, the group focus is different: low or high; inside or outside the group; to an invisible point in space or to an actual object or person.

What is your *reaction* to this? Might it change the subsequent mood of the conversations when they are resumed?

7.5 CREATING DIALOGUE

A

Suppose somebody said to you:

'Dad's giving me a red Ferrari next year.'

What motive could this person have for telling you this?

Discuss the following reactions to the same statement. What does each reveal about the speaker?

* Not likely. You're not old enough.
* Dad would buy one for me too. I've only got to ask.
* Why red? White's safer.
* Lucky you.
* How come?

Which of these reactions, if any, would help to build the conversation? Which would cut it off?

B

Decide on a possible response to one of the following conversation starters. Then work in pairs. A begins the conversation with one of the starters, B responds. Build the conversation in this way, remembering to *listen* to what your partner is saying.

a. It wouldn't be fair.
b. Remember the time when we . . .
c. But I'm only 18.
d. Congratulations. I just heard the news.

Discuss: the meaning of a conversation depends on more than the words.

C

Form groups of six and work in pairs on one of the following. Your object is to hold the conversation so that you make it clear what each person feels about the other.

The conversation in all three cases takes place in a car travelling to town.

* Husband and wife married 25 years.
* Two friends.
* Two people employed by the same firm.

Before you begin, decide what the attitude of each person is to the other, something about the character of each, and what the conversation might be about.

7.6 **IDENTIFICATION**

You have been working closely with a partner, building responses based on your interpretation of what your partner did and said and felt.

The process of identifying with a character enables us to see and respond to the world from that character's point of view. It is as if we were standing in another person's shoes.

In this section we shall work on simple ways of helping you to identify with a character you are going to play.

When asked on a recent TV show about where he gets his ideas for the comic characters he creates, Dick Emery, the British comedian said he worked from experience, from observations stored in memory. When he wanted to create a particular character, such as a tea lady or a bikie, he had mental pictures from which he could use a mannerism or a way of talking which would help him to develop a character.

When you are asked to play a character, it may help you to draw on your experience of life and people, if you make a kind of identikit of the character. You may then begin to see this character as a real person, quite distinct from yourself.

A *Making an Identikit*

When you have read the details of the storyline below, prepare an identikit for each of the characters as shown.

Storyline: A young person is pleading with his/her aunt and uncle to allow him/her to come and live with them. One of the relatives is unwilling. The other does not know what would be the best for everyone.

Young person

Name ....
Age .... Sex ....
Occupation ....
Height .... Weight ....
What has happened to lead to this request ....
....
....
How do I feel about Aunt, Uncle?
....
Where am I living now? ....
....
Other information ....
....

You now have a picture of three characters in a particular situation. Work in groups of three. Decide which character you will be, and study your identikit.

Begin playing the scene with the young person about to make the request. Continue the dialogue until the three characters have come to some decision.

After you have played the situation, discuss how closely your identikit reflected you character. Did you, for example, learn more about the character you were playing? If so, on what did this further information depend?

Try replaying the scene, using the identikits prepared by another group. Spend some time reading your new identikit. What is different about this character's walk or way of speaking?

When you have come to a decision in your second enactment, compare the solutions you found to the problem. Compare the ways in which you reached these solutions.

7.7 CHARACTERISATION

A *Visualising a character*

Becoming a character is a slow process. Sometimes it helps to visualise as the photographs do, the character you are playing at a particular time, or in a particular place, or doing a particular action.

Write down what the person in each of these photographs might be thinking.

What clues suggest your interpretation?

Interpret, in a similar way, the photographs on pages 6, 11, 16, 18, 21 & 22.

Read some of the monologues aloud. Remember you appear as the person in the photograph, and you are thinking aloud.

Discuss the differences you noticed in the mood or the personality of the characters in the different situations.

What made the differences?

B Character and Improvisation

Because character is important in determining what happens in a situation, you must know the character you are playing.

Develop the following improvisation in steps as suggested. What happens depends on the characters you create.

Scenario: The president of a charity committee is asking a TV star to make an appearance for charity at a public function.

a. Visualise the characters as individuals, not as stereotypes. Make identikits for both.

b. Work in pairs. Become one of the characters. Decide on a movement or a gesture that suits your character. How does your character walk? ... talk? If your imagination runs dry, try to picture your character as an animal or a bird. If, for example, your president is lively, you might work from a mental picture of something lively like a cricket or a wagtail. If your pop star is acquisitive, you might work from the movements of a magpie.

c. Set your scene. Where does it occur? Does the setting impose any strain on either character?

d. Decide how well your characters know each other. Which character begins the conversation? How does the other character react?
    Build the dialogue so that the reason for the end result (a *yes* or *no*) is made clear.

e. Show your work to the rest of the group.

f. Replay the scene, changing partners, and using a different location. Continue making your language suit the character you are developing. Does the way you speak change with the location?

7.8 DEVELOPING CONFLICT

When a conflict develops between two people, changes may occur in their attitudes to one another. There may, for example, be a slow build-up of tension before the problem is solved, and then a quick release of tension. The tension will affect the way the people react to one another.

A STORYLINES

In the following storylines, work to develop the conflict. Begin by answering the following questions about each conflict.

* How does the conflict begin?
* What is the involvement of each person?
* What feeds the conflict? Is it, for example, the attitude of one? of both?
* What solutions to the conflict are possible, given the time, place and characters?

Storyline 1: Work in pairs.

A dissatisfied customer is determined to return an article of clothing which has not been used. The shop assistant refuses to accept the article.

Remember that your actions reflect your intentions.

Work with another partner and replay the scene using different characters in different shops. What differences does each change make to the way the two persons approach each other? to the tone of voice? to the speed with which they find a solution?

Storyline 2: The scene is a main line railway station. A railway employer is sweeping the platform. A snobbish person insists on remaining seated where the employee wants to sweep.

Show the employee going through a number of steps in his/her approach—being, for example, polite, growing assertive and becoming angry. How do the actions of the seated person change?

Replay the scene. This time on the seat there is an unemployed person who missed out on getting a similar job with the Department of Railways. Begin by deciding who has the problem in this scene. What is the attitude of each person to the sweeping?

When you have played the scene, discuss how clearly the problem between the two persons was shown.

B

Developing conflict by introducing tension.

Sometimes somebody or something outside a situation introduces conflict. As you work on developing the storyline below, spend time on each step so you can make clear the changes that occur in each. The questions might help you focus.

One　A young technician and a friend are putting together some electronic equipment one Saturday afternoon when there is a knock at the door.

One　What are the friends talking about as they work? (Prepare an identikit for each.)

Two　Two policemen enter. They tell the technician that the owner of a house where he/she was working the previous week has accused him/her of stealing valuable tape-recording equipment. The technician denies this strongly. The police spend some time questioning before asking the technician to accompany them to the station for fingerprinting. The technician refuses, not wanting his/her prints to be on police files.

Two　Which police officer speaks first?
How does he/she state the problem?
What does the friend do during the interview?
What effect does the statement of the problem have on each friend?
Does the technician refuse to go immediately?
What is the attitude of the police to the refusal?

Three　The technician shuts the door as the police leave. The two friends talk things over. They plan what they will do if the police take further action.

Three　Decide if the technician is guilty or not. How does this affect his/her decision? How is the atmosphere different from that in Step i? What is the effect on their work? Act out the scene.

7.9 BUILDING A CLIMAX

We have been working on developing a scene by introducing conflict into it. Now we emphasise the building of the climax (the high point) in a scene.

Use the given steps in the following background story to build the climax.

A young girl has been blind since birth. Her parents hear of a surgeon abroad who is having some success operating on similar cases. The operation is delicate, but the parents decide to take a last chance to help their daughter to see. The surgeon operates. The day comes when the bandages are to be removed. The girl asks for permission to remove the bandages herself.

Storyline:

One   The girl asks permission to take off the bandages.

Two   The girl is left alone in the room and begins to take off the bandages.

Pay particular attention to using non-verbal elements here, e.g. After the girl is left alone, how long is it before she begins? Are her movements slow or rapid? What variations are there in the speed of her movements?

Three It is getting dark. The girl screams. You must decide the reason for the scream.

When you are satisfied with the way you have built the climax, devise an ending. This may be brief, but will make clear the reason for the scream.

7.10 STRUCTURING IMPROVISATION

The focus in this section is on building improvisation, using four different kinds of stimuli for ideas.

When you have worked through this section, choose some of your own source material from which to make improvisations.

A *Developing an improvisation from a photograph.*

a. What conflicts does this photograph suggest to you? In groups, work out what events might have led to the incident recorded in the photograph. What people were involved? Where was the photographer?

Write down the order of the events that you think immediately preceded the taking of the photograph. Taking the parts of the people involved, act the sequence. Look at the work of your group critically. Is your explanation of the photograph believable?

Rehearse the 30 seconds before the camera clicked, so that you can make the movement sequence accurate. When you are in the position of the three in the photograph, use dialogue to reveal what is happening. What is the problem each of you is facing? Who is speaking? Improvise the dialogue until the moment when the three change their positions. Move to the new position.

Show your work to the other groups and discuss how clear each of you made the reasons for your changes of movement. How well did the words of each group suit the situation? the characters who said them?

b. Form three groups. One person in each group chooses one of the characters in the photograph. Together, work out a scene that shows this character at 6 o'clock on the evening the photograph was taken. Where is the character? What is his attitude to the events of the day? Who is he with? What is his relationship with the person or persons? What particular problem is he facing now? Show what happens, making your words and actions suit your character and the situation.

When you have had time to discuss the details of your scene and bring it to life, compare the behaviour of each of the three persons in the photograph with his behaviour at 6. How different was the 6 o'clock world to that of the photograph? What made any difference?

This story is an updated version of a biblical story, *The Good Samaritan.*

INCIDENT ON HIGHWAY 31

At closing time, a young man travelling from Sydney to Melbourne on his motor cycle, left the bar where he had had a few drinks. It was raining, and in the dark he missed a bend in the road.

He lay in pain until he saw the headlights of a truck approaching. He struggled to sit up to attract the driver's attention. But the driver, anxious to deliver his load on time, passed by without seeing him.

The young man staggered to his feet. He wiped the blood from his eyes, and fell against a road post, against which he propped himself to wait for help.

A car picked up the slumped figure in its headlights. It slowed down and he heard a woman's voice:

"No, don't stop. Teach him a lesson. These drunks get all they deserve."

The driver accelerated, and the young man, his strength gone, fell to the ground where passing motorists did not see him.

Some time later, a hitchhiker carrying pack and guitar walked along the road. She passed the bike and when she saw the young man she stopped, took off her wind-jacket and covered him with it as best she could. Then as a car approached, she stepped into the middle of the road, signalling the driver to stop.

The car swerved to avoid her and almost ran over the young man lying still by the roadside.

"Unemployed bludger. A woman would be mad to pick up anyone like that at night. You might never get to work the next day."

The woman's companion agreed.

"As it is, we don't have time for unscheduled stops if we're going to get to work on time. You can't drive fast in this weather."

The hitchhiker ran back to the young man to move him onto the grass, and as she bent over, a police cycle stopped.

"What's the trouble?" the policeman asked.

"A cyclist has been hurt," she said.

After calling an ambulance, the policeman flagged down a passing car driven by a clergyman.

"Will you give this hitchhiker a lift to the all-night café up the road? She looks as if she could do with a coffee. I'll be along presently."

The clergyman drove the hitchhiker to the café. The occupants of the cars that had refused to stop were finishing a hot snack.

The clergyman nodded to them and they returned the greeting.

"Not too nice out to-night, is it?" said one.

The hitchhiker stood inside the door and her voice was sharp.

"No, not too nice to be out."

They stared as she moved to the table.

To simplify dramatising the story, we suggest using three scenes to correspond to the three places in which the action takes place.

Scene one: The pub.
Scene two: On the road.
Scene three: The all-night café.

Decide what character you will play and make an identikit. Picture your character clearly—the age of the character; the way the character talks and moves; the reasons for travel; and so on.

Choose the characters you need, altering the number to suit the group. Each group works on one of the following scenes.

Scene one: People drinking, joking, talking.
                 Musicians.
                 Young man and friends.
                 Licensee and people behind the bar.

Scene two: Young man.
                 Truck driver.
                 Hitchhiker.
                 Four persons in cars.
                 Policeman.

Scene three: Proprietor of café and employees.
                 Four people from cars.
                 Truck driver.
                 Clergyman.
                 Hitchhiker.

When you have finished preparing your characters, set up each scene, in a different area of the room, using the details below as the basis for developing the atmosphere, the dialogue and the movement. When you are ready, put the three scenes together as a play.

The Play

Scene one: The bar. 9.00 p.m.

It is not long until closing time and everyone is having a good time. There is music, some singing and joking, and the bar is kept busy. The young man is not drinking much. He says he has to leave and the others warn him about driving safely. He laughs and tells them he has never had an accident. As he leaves, someone warns him about police cycle patrols.

Scenes two and three:

Work out the details for these scenes. Pay particular attention to building a strong ending in which the hitchhiker has the last word.

75

Developing an improvisation from a play, *Spoon River Anthology*
by Edgar Lee Masters

In these extracts, the dead in the Spoon River graveyard have come to life to tell
something about themselves and about each other.

Albert Schirding

Jonas Keene thought his lot a hard one
Because his children were all failures.
But I know of a fate more trying than that:
It is to be a failure while your children are successes.
For I raised a brood of eagles
Who flew away at last, leaving me
A crow on the abandoned bough.
Then, with the ambition to prefix Honorable to my name,
And thus to win my children's admiration,
I ran for County Superintendent of Schools,
spending my accumulations to win—and lost.
That fall my daughter received first prize in Paris
For her picture, entitled, "The Old Mill"—
(It was of the water mill before Henry Wilkin put in steam.)
The feeling that I was not worthy of her finished me.

Jonas Keene

Why did Albert Schirding kill himself
Trying to be County Superindendent of Schools,
Blest as he was with the means of life
And wonderful children, bringing him honor
Ere he was sixty?
If even one of my boys could have run a news-stand,
Or one of my girls could have married a decent man,
I should not have walked in the rain
And jumped into bed with clothes all wet,
Refusing medical aid.

Judge Selah Lively

Suppose you stood just five feet two,
And had worked your way as a grocery clerk,
Studying law by candle light
Until you became an attorney at law?
And then suppose through your diligence,
And regular church attendance,
You became attorney for Thomas Rhodes,
Collecting notes and mortgages,
And representing all the widows
In the Probate Court? And through it all
They jeered at your size, and laughed at your clothes
And your polished boots? And then suppose
You became the County Judge?
And Jefferson Howard and Kinsey Keene,
And Harmon Whitney, and all the giants
Who had sneered at you, were forced to stand
Before the bar and say "Your Honor"—
Well, don't you think it was natural
That I made it hard for them?

What information does Albert Schirding give about himself?

How does he compare himself with Jonas Keene?

What do Jonas Keene's words add to our picture of Albert?

What is Jonas' feeling towards his children?

In pairs, using the information you have about the characters in the *Spoon River* extracts, build scenes that might have happened between—

a. Jonas and one of his children:

What does Jonas want from this child? (i.e. what is the problem?)
What is his attitude to the child?
What is the child's feeling towards Jonas? How old is the child when this scene you are building takes place?
Where does it happen?
What change could this scene have on the relationship between father and child?

b. Jonas and his child's teacher in the primary school.

Why does the teacher want to talk to Jonas?
How does the teacher feel about this school? about children? about Jonas' child?

Work to show the characters of the two people in action at the beginning of the scene. Decide, for example, how this teacher will greet Jonas; broach the subject; listen to Jonas.

c. Mr and Mrs Keene discuss a particular problem they have with one of their children.

Why is finding a solution to this problem important to them? What is the attitude of each to the child? How would you describe the relationship between Mr and Mrs Keene? Are they, for example, used to talking things out?

Set up the scene before you work on dialogue.

d. Albert Schirding and his wife.

Problem: Albert wants to run for the job of country superintendent. His wife opposes this.

What does this suggest to you about Mrs Schirding's values? About Albert's nature? How would Albert broach the subject to his wife? How does she respond at first? Is she, for example, used to being consulted about similar problems? At what stage does Albert make it clear he intends to go ahead? What is Mrs Schirding's response?

Judge Selah Lively is another of the Spoon River dead. From your reading of his words, what do you think is important in motivating him? Could this be a problem for him?

In appropriately sized groups, choose one of the following situations to develop as an improvisation to show to the other groups.

a. Mr Lively asserts himself.

What is the occasion? . . . public or private? Is the matter on which Mr Lively asserts himself important or not? In what ways (verbal and non-verbal) does Mr Lively assert himself? Does his assertion become aggressive? What response does he arouse? How much do you think Mr Lively's name might be a reflection of his personality? How would you show this?

b. Judge Lively asserts himself. Who would be present?

How can you set up a court? Who might Judge Lively assert his authority against? How might he deal with opposition? What effect might he have on others in court?

c. Selah Lively, aged 12, asserts himself.

Who provoked Selah so he feels he must assert himself? What does he learn from this encounter? What does the other character learn about Selah? Who else is present? What effect does the incident have on onlookers?

Developing improvisation and other activities from a poem. *Dooley is a Traitor* by James Michie.

The attitudes of the characters are important.
Read the poem and decide what the poet's attitude is to Dooley and to the Judge?
What is Dooley's attitude to the Judge? . . . and the Judge's to Dooley?

"So then you won't fight?"
"Yes, your Honor," I said, "that's right."
"Now is it that you simply aren't willing,
Or have you a fundamental moral objection to killing?"
Says the judge, blowing his nose.
And making his words stand to attention in long rows.
I stand to attention too, but with half a grin
(In my time I've done a good many in).
"No objection at all, sir," I said.
"There's a deal of the world I'd rather see dead—
Such as Johnny Stubbs or Fred Settle or my last landlord, Mr. Syme.
Give me a gun and your blessing, your Honor, and I'll be killing them all
    the time.
But my conscience says a clear no
To killing a crowd of gentlemen I don't know.
Why, I'd as soon think of killing a worshipful judge,
High-court, like yourself (against whom, God knows, I've got no grudge—
So far), as murder a heap of foreign folk.
If you've got no grudge, you've got no joke
To laugh at after."
                    Now the words never come flowing
Proper for me till I get the old pipe going.
And just as I was poking.
Down baccy, the judge looks up sharp with "No smoking,
Mr. Dooley. We're not fighting this war for fun.
And we want a clearer reason why you refuse to carry a gun.
This war is not a personal feud, it's a fight
Against wrong ideas on behalf of the Right.
Mr. Dooley, won't you help to destroy evil ideas?"
"Ah, your Honor, here's
The tragedy," I said. "I'm not a man of the mind.
I couldn't find it in my heart to be unkind
To an idea. I wouldn't know one if I saw one. I haven't one of my own.
So I'd best be leaving other people's alone."

"Indeed," he sneers at me, "this defense is
Curious for someone with convictions in two senses.
A criminal invokes conscience to his aid
To support an individual withdrawal from a communal crusade
Sanctioned by God, led by the Church, against a godless, churchless nation!"
I asked his Honor for a translation.
"You talk of conscience," he said. "What do you know of the Christian creed?"
"Nothing, sir, except what I can read,
That's the most you can hope for from us jailbirds.
I just open the Book here and there and look at the words.
And I find when the Lord himself misliked an evil notion
He turned it into a pig and drove it squealing over a cliff into the ocean,
And the loony ran away
And lived to think another day.
There was a clean job done and no blood shed!
Everybody happy and forty wicked thoughts drowned dead.
A neat and Christian murder. None of your mad slaughter
Throwing away the brains with the blood and the baby with the bathwater.
Now I look at the war as a sportsman. It's a matter of choosing
The decentest way of losing.
Heads or tails, losers or winners,
We all lose, we're all damned sinners.
And I'd rather be with the poor cold people at the wall that's shot
Than the bloody guilty devils in the firing line, in Hell and keeping hot."
"But what right, Dooley, what right," he cried,
"Have you to say the Lord is on your side?"
"That's a dirty crooked question," back I roared.
"I said not the Lord was on my side, but I was on the side of the Lord."
Then he was up at me and shouting,
But by and by he calms: "Now we're not doubting
Your sincerity, Dooley, only your arguments,
Which don't make sense."
("Hullo," I thought, "that's the wrong way round.
I may be skylarking a bit, but my brainpan's sound.")
Then biting his nail and sugaring his words sweet:
"Keep your head, Mr. Dooley. Religion is clearly not up your street.
But let me ask you as a plain patriotic fellow
Whether you'd stand there so smug and yellow
If the foe were attacking your own dear sister."
"I'd knock their brains out, mister,
On the floor," I said. "There," he says kindly, "I knew you were no pacifist
It's your straight duty as a man to enlist.

The enemy is at the door." You could have downed
Me with a feather. "Where?" I gasp, looking round.
"Not this door," he says angered. "Don't play the clown.
But they're two thousand miles away planning to do us down.
Why, the news is full of the deeds of those murderers and rapers."
"Your Eminence," I said, "my father told me never to believe the papers
But to go by my eyes,
And at two thousand miles the poor things can't tell the truth from lies."
His fearful spectacles glittered like the moon: "For the last time what right
Has a man like you to refuse to fight?"
"More right," I said, "than you.
You've never murdered a man, so you don't know what it is I won't do.
I've done it in good hot blood, so haven't I the right to make bold
To declare that I shan't do it in cold?"
Then the judge rises in a great rage
And writes DOOLEY IS A TRAITOR in black upon a page
And tells me I must die.
"What, me?" says I.
"If you still won't fight."
"Well, yes, your Honor," I said, "that's right."

a. Dooley is shown as having a number of *faces*—among them clown, jail-bird, sportsman and brother.
   Complete the list of other *faces* which Dooley might have.
   Work in twos or threes to make a mask out of thin cardboard which will identify one of the *faces* of Dooley. Use the sketch of simple masks as a guide. Paint Dooley's *face* on the mask, or use junk like plastic pieces and remnants of material to give an impression of the *face*.

Each of the *faces* of Dooley might give a different, although a truthful answer to questions about him.

Build a complete picture of Dooley as follows:
Form two circles, one inside the other. Those who play the different *faces* of Dooley make the inside circle, and wear or hold the appropriate mask. Those in the outside circle ask questions which will build a picture of the man, Dooley. Two people might be recorders to compile information.
Ask each question in a set form (a ritual), as:
*   Jail-bird Dooley, what happened when you left prison?
*   Brother Dooley, how well did you get on with your sister?

Everyone has a turn in each circle. Ask other questions of other faces.

b. Choose one of the following lines taken from the text and, using the questions below, use it as the basis for an improvisation to be presented to the other group.
*   *There was a clean job done and no bloodshed.*
*   *Then he was up at me and shouting.*

Use the line you select as part of an original story your group makes up. Decide where the line occurs in your story . . . the opening? . . . the climax? . . . the end? . . . who says the line, and what happened just before the line was spoken. Work out the details of your story, and decide who plays the parts. Discuss the shaping of your improvisations as you work. Write down the storyline.
What is the lead-in? the conflict? the climax? the solution?

8 APPLICATION

The aim of this chapter is to work on text to bring it to life by consciously applying the perceptions and skills you have been developing. You may want to stage your work for an audience or you may want to increase your understanding of the script.

In working on each script, set up the scene using simple props you might find in your classroom, with perhaps one piece of costume to help you get the feel of the part you play.

Here are some of the ways in which plays are presented. Your way will depend of course on the space and the facilities at your disposal.

Stage directions are always taken from the actor's position.

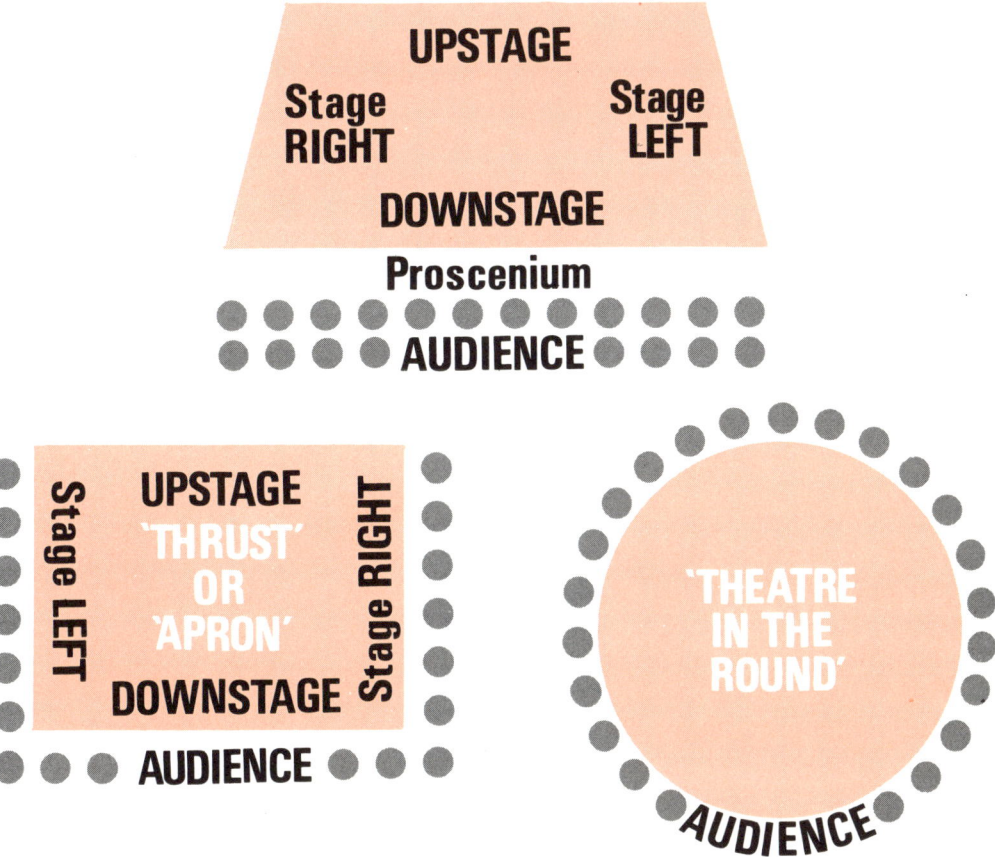

8.1 From PICNIC by William Inge, Act Two

Madge and Millie are sisters. Madge, the elder, is beautiful and engaged to be married. Millie is shy, a tomboy. The scene takes place in front of their house. What does Millie want from Madge? . . . and what is Madge's attitude to her? Their movement and their stillness should tell us something about their inner and outer conflicts.

It is late afternoon, the same day. The sun is beginning to set and fills the atmosphere with radiant orange. When the curtain goes up, Millie is on the porch alone. She has permitted herself to "dress up" and wears a becoming, feminine dress in which she cannot help feeling a little strange. She is quite attractive. Piano music can be heard off stage, somewhere past Mrs. Potts' house, and Millie stands listening to it for a moment. Then she begins to sway to the music and in a moment is dancing a strange, impromptu dance over the porch and yard. The music stops suddenly and Millie's mood is broken. She rushes upstage and calls off, left.

MILLIE. Don't quit now Ernie! (*She cannot hear Ernie's reply*) Huh? (*Madge enters from kitchen. Millie turns to Madge*) Ernie's waiting for the rest of the band to practice. They're going to play out at the park tonight.

MADGE. (*crossing to center and sitting on chair.*) I don't know why you couldn't have helped us in the kitchen.

MILLIE. (*lightly, giving her version of the sophisticated belle.*) I had to dress for the ball.

MADGE. I had to make the potato salad and stuff the eggs and make three dozen bread-and-butter sandwiches.

MILLIE. (*in a very affected accent.*) I had to *bathe*—and dust my limbs with powder—and slip into my frock . . .

MADGE. Did you clean out the bathtub?

MILLIE. Yes, I cleaned out the bathtub. (*She becomes very selfconscious*) Madge, how do I look? Now tell me the truth.

MADGE. You look very pretty.

MILLIE. I feel sorta funny.

MADGE. You can have the dress if you want it.

MILLIE. Thanks. (*A pause*) Madge, how do you talk to boys?

MADGE. Why, you just talk, silly.

MILLIE. How d'ya think of things to say?

MADGE. I don't know. You just say whatever comes into your head.

MILLIE. Supposing nothing ever comes into my head?

MADGE. You talked with him all right this morning.

MILLIE. But now I've got a *date* with him, and it's *different!*

MADGE. You're crazy.

MILLIE. I think he's a big show-off. You should have seen him this morning on the high diving board. He did real graceful swan dives, and a two and a half gainer, and a back flip—and kids stood around clapping. He just ate it up.

MADGE. (*her mind elsewhere.*) I think I'll paint my toenails tonight and wear sandals.

MILLIE. And he was braggin' all afternoon how he used to be a deep-sea diver off Catalina Island.

MADGE. Honest?

MILLIE. And he says he used to make hundreds of dollars doin' parachute jumps out of a balloon. Do you believe it?

MADGE. I don't see why not.

MILLIE. You never hear Alan bragging that way.

MADGE. Alan never jumped out of a balloon.

MILLIE. Madge, I think he's girl crazy.

MADGE. You think every boy you see is something horrible.

MILLIE. Alan took us into the Hi Ho for Cokes and there was a gang of girls in the back booth—Juanita Badger and her gang. (*Madge groans at hearing this name*) When they saw him, they started giggling and tee-heeing and saying all sorts of crazy things. Then Juanita Badger comes up to me and whispers, "He's the cutest thing I ever saw." Is he, Madge?

MADGE. (*not willing to go overboard.*) I certainly wouldn't say he was "the cutest thing I ever *saw*."

MILLIE. Juanita Badger's an old floozy. She sits in the back row at the movie so the guys that come in will see her and sit with her. One time she and Rubberneck Krauss were asked by the management to leave—and they weren't just kissin', either!

MADGE. (*proudly.*) I never even speak to Juanita Badger.

MILLIE. Madge, do you think he'll like me?

MADGE. Why ask me all these questions? You're supposed to be the smart one.

MILLIE. I don't really care. I just wonder.

Experiment with different ways of setting up this scene. Which makes it easier for Millie to show off her dress? Move away from Madge? Become the centre of interest?

Which arrangement might mean that one character is talking upstage (i.e. away from the audience, so the audience cannot see her face, nor hear her clearly.)

Experiment with different ways of setting your scene so that the two characters will make interesting contrasting pictures as one or both move.

Where is your audience? How does this affect where and how your characters position themselves?

One group might prefer to tape the dialogue as a segment from a radio play, with music and sound effects.

8.2 From THE ZOO STORY by Edward Albee.

In the beginning of the play, Albee is developing a conflict between two people in Central Park. He is specific about the way the scene should look.

Read the extract, book in hand, moving as the text requires. Which character has a problem? Who is the more aggressive character?

THE PLAYERS

PETER. *A man in his early forties, neither fat nor gaunt, neither handsome nor homely. He wears tweeds, smokes a pipe, carries horn-rimmed glasses. Although he is moving into middle age, his dress and his manner would suggest a man younger.*

JERRY. *A man in his late thirties, not poorly dressed, but carelessly. What was once a trim and lightly muscled body has begun to go to fat; and while he is no longer handsome, it is evident that he once was. His fall from physical grace should not suggest debauchery; he has, to come closest to it, a great weariness.*

The Scene: It is Central Park; a Sunday afternoon in summer; the present. There are two park benches, one toward either side of the stage; they both face the audience. Behind them: foliage, trees, sky. At the beginning, Peter is seated on one of the benches.

(Stage Directions: As the curtain rises, Peter is seated on the bench stage-right. He is reading a book. He stops reading, cleans his glasses, goes back to reading. Jerry enters.)

JERRY. I've been to the zoo. (PETER *doesn't notice.*) I said, I've been to the zoo. MISTER, I'VE BEEN TO THE ZOO!

PETER. Hm?... What?... I'm sorry, were you talking to me?

JERRY. I went to the zoo, and then I walked until I came here. Have I been walking north?

PETER. (*puzzled.*) North? Why... I... I think so. Let me see.

JERRY. (*pointing past the audience*.) Is that Fifth Avenue?

PETER. Why yes; it is.

JERRY. And what is that cross street there; that one, to the right?

PETER. That? Oh, that's Seventy-Fourth Street.

JERRY. And the zoo is around Sixty-Fifth Street; so, I've been walking north.

PETER. (*anxious to get back to his reading.*) Yes; it would seem so.

JERRY.   Good old north.

PETER.   (*lightly, by reflex.*) Ha, ha.

JERRY.   (*after a slight pause.*) But not due north.

PETER.   I . . . well, no, not due north; but, we . . . call it north. It's northerly.

JERRY.   (*watches as* PETER, *anxious to dismiss him, prepares his pipe.*) Well, boy; *you're* not going to get lung cancer, are you?

PETER.   (*looks up, a little annoyed, then smiles.*) No sir. Not from this.

JERRY.   No, sir. What you'll probably get is cancer of the mouth, and then you'll have to wear one of those things Freud wore after they took one whole side of his jaw away. What do they call those things?

PETER.   (*uncomfortable.*) A prosthesis?

JERRY.   The very thing! A prosthesis. You're an educated man, aren't you? Are you a doctor?

PETER.   Oh, no; no. I read about it somewhere; *Time* magazine I think. (*He turns to his book.*)

JERRY.   Well, *Time* magazine isn't for blockheads.

PETER.   No. I suppose not.

JERRY.   (*after a pause.*) Boy, I'm glad that's Fifth Avenue there.

PETER.   (*vaguely.*) Yes.

JERRY.   I don't like the west side of the park much.

PETER.   Oh? (*Then, slightly wary, but interested*) Why?

JERRY.   (*offhand.*) I don't know.

PETER.   Oh. (*He returns to his book.*)

JERRY.   (*He stands for a few seconds, looking at* PETER, *who finally looks up again, puzzled.*) Do you mind if we talk?

PETER.   (*obviously minding.*) Why . . . no, no.

JERRY.   Yes you do; you do.

PETER.   (*puts his book down, his pipe out and away, smiling.*) No, really; I don't mind.

JERRY.   Yes you do.

PETER.   (*finally decided.*) No; I don't mind at all, really.

JERRY.   It's . . . it's a nice day.

PETER.   (*stares unnecessarily at the sky.*) Yes. Yes, it is; lovely.

After discussion, improvise the scene without the text.

To give you ideas for developing the reaction between Jerry and Peter, work in pairs. One of you is reading (aloud?) from a book, the other is determined to distract you. No physical contact is allowed. Concentrate on either distracting or not being distracted. Use some of these improvised movements to help you to interpret the text.

Use your own words and movements to show the changing conflict between Jerry and Peter. How does this give the scene a shape. Contrast one character moving with the other character still. What feeling between Jerry and Peter did your own words convey?

Can you transfer this to the text?

Re-read the scene, giving attention to:
* Timing Jerry's entry. How long is Peter alone on the stage?
* Moving Jerry so that he prevents Peter reading without invading Peter's space.

Try working in groups of three; two actors and a director, who observes and guides them.

Continue the process of going back to the text and discussing ideas for developing your interpretation until you are satisfied with what you have done.

8.3 From OH WHAT A LOVELY WAR.

This is a scene from a play which was developed through improvisation by the Theatre Workshop and Charles Chilton under the direction of Joan Littlewood. The title of the play is ironic.
(*M.C.: Master of Ceremonies*)

The M.C. comes in and sets a stand for Mrs Pankhurst. During the following scene he wanders round the stage as a silent observer. Mrs Pankhurst and a crowd of bystanders come on. As she climbs on her box the crowd whistle.

FIRST MAN. 1 Shut up!

MRS PANKHURST.   Now, before talking to you all, I should like to read you a letter from my friend George Bernard Shaw.

SECOND MAN.   Who's he when he's at home?

FIRST WOMAN.   Ain't it disgusting?

MRS PANKHURST.   He says: 'The men of this country are being sacrificed to the blunders of boobies, the cupidity of capitalists, the ambition of conquerors, the lusts and lies and rancours of bloodthirsts that love war, because it opens their prison doors and sets them on the throne of power and popularity.'

THIRD MAN.   Now give us a song!

MRS PANKHURST.   For the second time peace is being offered to the sorely tried people of the civilized world . . .

SECOND MAN.   Hallo.

MRS PANKHURST. . . . at the close of 1915 President Wilson proposed an immediate armistice; to be followed by a peace conference . . .

SECOND MAN.   Hallo!

MRS PANKHURST. . . . in April of this year, Germany herself proposed peace . . .

SECOND MAN.   Hallo! Hallo!

MRS PANKHURST. . . . the peace movements are strong in England, France and the United States; and in Germany. In the Reichstag . . .

SECOND MAN.   Who's he when he's at home?

MRS PANKHURST. . . . the peace groups are active and outspoken; the exact terms of Germany's offer have never been made known to us and I should like to ask Lloyd George what his war aims are.

FIRST WOMAN.   I should like to ask you what your old man has for dinner!

MRS PANKHURST. . . . the politicians chatter like imbeciles while civilization bleeds to death.

THIRD MAN.   You're talking like a traitor. Pacifists are traitors.

MRS PANKHURST.   I ask that gentleman . . .

THIRD MAN.   Don't ask me . . . 'Cos I don't know nothing . . . I'm stupid.

MRS PANKHURST. . . . to consider the plight of the civilized world after another year: you do not know what you do and the statesmen wash their hands of the whole affair . . .

FOURTH MAN.   Why don't you wash your face!

SECOND MAN.   Douglas Haig's got them on the run.

MRS PANKHURST.   Who tells you this? *The Times* . . .

SECOND MAN.   He's got them going.

MRS PANKHURST. . . . the newspaper that refuses to publish the pacifist letters, and distorts the facts of our so-called victories. We are killing off slowly but surely the best of the male population . . .

FIRST WOMAN.   Here! Don't you address them words to me . . .

SECOND WOMAN.   Here! Don't you address them words to her . . .

MRS PANKHURST. . . . the sons of Europe are being crucified . . .

FIRST WOMAN. . . . my old man's at the front . . .

SECOND WOMAN.   She's had her share of suffering . . .

MRS PANKHURST. . . . on the barbed wire, because you . . .

FIRST WOMAN.   Here, don't you address them words to me; my old man's at the front.

MRS PANKHURST. . . . you the misguided masses are crying out for it.

SECOND WOMAN.   Her old man's at the front.

FIRST WOMAN.   My old man's at the front.

MRS PANKHURST.   War cannot be won. No one can win a war. Is it your wish this war will go on and on until Germany is beaten to the ground?

NEWSPANEL. JULY 1 . . . SOMME . . . BRITISH LOSS 60,000 MEN ON THE FIRST DAY.

CROWD.   Yes! Yes!

They drown her with shouts. They sing.

SONG.   RULE, BRITANNIA
Rule, Britannia, Britannia rules the waves,
Britons, never, never, never, shall be slaves.
Rule, Britannia, Britannia rules the waves,
Britons never, never, never shall . . .

Two drunken soldiers come on as the crowd goes off, and sing.

There are people in the crowd who do not have lines to say. Each of these people should take a definite attitude towards the proceedings—hostile? amused? indifferent? Each person's behaviour should be consistent throughout the scene.

How much is the crowd reacting to the sex of the speaker? . . . the choice of words? . . . the point of view?

What device would serve for the panel? What is the function of the news item here?

Maintaining pace is important. Mrs Pankhurst's words and those of the crowd must be heard clearly despite the interjections.

What kind of woman does Mrs Pankhurst appear to be? How can her qualities be brought out—in her posture? . . . gestures? . . . voice? What effect do the interjections have, for example, on her voice?

The song is the crowd's answer to Mrs Pankhurst's question. How should it be sung?

8.4 From AN ENEMY OF THE PEOPLE by Henrik Ibsen

In Act IV of this play a public meeting takes place. Dr Stockmann has discovered that the public baths are a source of dangerous pollution and should be closed. Dr Stockmann's brother, Peter, the mayor, and important citizens like Aslaksen, oppose Dr Stockmann because the town depends on the baths to bring tourists and prosperity to the town.

Read the text around the class to get an idea of the characters and tensions before you cast the play.

Ibsen has specified that the stage be set up in a particular way. Give some thought to the use you will make of the setting and the properties during the public meeting.

Reading Ibsen's stage directions, carefully use cut out paper shapes on squared paper to show the setting prescribed.

As there are a large number of people on stage, you might like to place some of them in the audience, as would happen in a public meeting. Work out entrances and seating for individuals at the meeting.

The text has been divided into sections to make it easy for you to follow a process of rehearsal followed by discussion and further rehearsal.

ACT IV

SCENE—*A big, old-fashioned room in* CAPTAIN HORSTER'S *house. At the back folding-doors, which are standing open, lead to an ante-room. Three windows in the left-hand wall. In the middle of the opposite wall a platform has been erected. On this is a small table with two candles, a water-bottle and glass, and a bell. The room is lit by lamps placed between the windows. In the fore-ground on the left there is a table with candles and a chair. To the right is a door and some chairs standing near it. The room is nearly filled with a crowd of townspeople of all sorts, a few women and schoolboys being amongst them. People are still streaming in from the back, and the room is soon filled.*

Section One

If you are playing one of the citizens, read all your lines in the text, or find places in the text where your reactions are important.

Build your identikit.

What is your age? education? occupation?

Why are you at the meeting?

What is your attitude to Dr Stockmann? to Peter Stockmann?

to the newspaper?

Where are your friends sitting?

What is your particular involvement in the issue of the meeting?

What information must the citizens communicate in this unit?

What is their mood?—It is important to establish this so we can follow the change in mood during the meeting.

1ST CITIZEN.   [*meeting another.*] Hullo, Lamstad! You here too?

2ND CITIZEN.   I go to every public meeting, I do.

3RD CITIZEN.   Brought your whistle too, I expect!

2ND CITIZEN.   I should think so. Haven't you?

3RD CITIZEN.   Rather! And old Evansen said he was going to bring a cowhorn, he did.

2ND CITIZEN.   Good old Evansen!
[*Laughter among the crowd.*]

5TH CITIZEN.   [*coming up to them*]. I say, tell me what is going on here to-night.

2ND CITIZEN.   Dr Stockmann is going to deliver an address attacking the Mayor.

4TH CITIZEN.   But the Mayor is his brother.

1ST CITIZEN.   That doesn't matter; Dr Stockmann's not the chap to be afraid.

3RD CITIZEN.   But he is in the wrong; it said so in the "People's Messenger".

2ND CITIZEN.   Yes, I expect he must be in the wrong this time, because neither the House-holders' Association nor the Citizens' Club would lend him their hall for his meeting.

1ST CITIZEN.   He couldn't even get the loan of the hall at the Baths.

2ND CITIZEN.   No, I should think not.

A MAN IN ANOTHER PART OF THE CROWD.   I say—who are we to back up in this?

92

ANOTHER MAN beside him. Watch Aslaksen, and do as he does.

BILL. [*pushing his way through the crowd, with a writing-case under his arm.*] Excuse me, gentlemen—do you mind letting me through? I am reporting for the "People's Messenger". Thank you very much! [*He sits down at the table on the left.*]

A WORKMAN. Who was that?

SECOND WORKMAN. Don't you know him? It's Billing, who writes for Aslaksen's paper.

[CAPTAIN HORSTER *brings in* MRS STOCKMANN *and* PETRA *through the door on the right.* EJLIF *and* MORTEN *follow them in.*]

HORS. I thought you might all sit here; you can slip out easily from here, if things get too lively.

MRS STO. Do you think there will be a disturbance?

HORS. One can never tell—with such a crowd. But sit down, and don't be uneasy.

MRS STO. [*sitting down.*] It was extremely kind of you to offer my husband the room.

HORS. Well, if nobody else would—

PETRA. [*who has sat down beside her mother.*] And it was a plucky thing to do, Captain Horster.

HORS. Oh, it is not such a great matter as all that.

[HOVSTAD *and* ASLAKSEN *make their way through the crowd.*]

ASL. [*going up to* HORSTER]. Has the Doctor not come yet?

HORS. He is waiting in the next room. [*Movement in the crowd by the door at the back.*]

HOV. Look—here comes the Mayor!

BILL. Yes, I'm damned if he hasn't come after all!

[PETER STOCKMANN *makes his way gradually through the crowd, bows courteously, and takes up a position by the wall on the left. Shortly afterwards* DR STOCKMANN *comes in by the right-hand door. He is dressed in a black frock-coat, with a white tie. There is a little feeble applause, which is hushed down. Silence is obtained.*]

Section Two

Supporters of Dr Stockmann and his brother take up their positions.

How will you change the focus from the citizens to each group of new arrivals in turn?

How does each character walk? . . . sit?

What kind of relationship do you think Dr and Mrs Stockmann have?

How will Mrs Stockmann reinforce her words with gestures and movements when she warns her husband?

DR STO. [*in an undertone.*] How do you feel, Katherine?

MRS STO. All right, thank you. [*Lowering her voice.*] Be sure not to lose your temper, Thomas.

DR STO. Oh, I know how to control myself. [*Looks at his watch, steps on to the platform, and bows.*] It is a quarter past—so I will begin. [*Takes his MS out of his pocket.*]

ASL. I think we ought to elect a chairman first.

DR STO. No, it is quite unnecessary.

SOME OF THE CROWD9 Yes—yes!

PETER. I certainly think too that we ought to have a chairman.

DR STO. But I have called this meeting to deliver a lecture, Peter.

PETER. Dr Stockmann's lecture may possibly lead to a considerable conflict of opinion.

VOICES IN THE CROWD9 A chairman! A chairman!

HOV. The general wish of the meeting seems to be that a chairman should be elected.

DR STO. [*restraining himself.*] Very well—let the meeting have its way.

ASL. Will the Mayor be good enough to undertake the task?

THREE MEN. [*clapping their hands.*] Bravo! Bravo!

PETER. For various reasons, which you will easily understand, I must beg to be excused. But fortunately we have amongst us a man who I think will be acceptable to you all. I refer to the President of the Householders' Association, Mr Aslaksen.

SEVERAL VOICES. Yes—Aslaksen! Bravo Aslaksen!

[DR STOCKMANN *takes up his MS and walks up and down the platform.*]

ASL. Since my fellow-citizens choose to entrust me with this duty, I cannot refuse.

[*Loud applause.* ASLAKSEN *mounts the platform.*]

BILL. [*writing.*] "Mr Aslaksen was elected with enthusiasm."

Section Four

What do Aslaksen's speeches reveal about his character? his values? his ability to think?

What is the significance of Aslaksen, as chairman, making his remarks?

Aslaksen is President of the Householder's Association.

You may know someone whose mannerisms or voice inflections you can use as a model for working on the way Aslaksen speaks.

What are the ways in which a speaker signals he expects a reaction from the crowd?

Peter and Aslaksen support each other. Do their positions on stage make this obvious?

Section Five

Will Peter move before he speaks?

What is Peter's purpose? Is he appealing to reason? to emotion? What is his tone of voice? What phrases does he stress in his speech?

ASL. And now, as I am in this position, I should like to say a few brief words. I am a quiet and peaceable man, who believes in discreet moderation, and—and—in moderate discretion. All my friends can bear witness to that.

SEVERAL VOICES. That's right! That's right, Aslaksen!

ASL. I have learnt in the school of life and experience that moderation is the most valuable virtue a citizen can possess—

PETER. Hear, hear!

ASL. And moreover that discretion and moderation are what enable a man to be of most service to the community. I would therefore suggest to our esteemed fellow-citizen, who has called this meeting, that he should strive to keep strictly within the bounds of moderation.

A MAN BY THE DOOR. Three cheers for the Moderation Society!

A VOICE. Shame!

SEVERAL VOICES. Sh!—Sh!

ASL. No interruptions, gentlemen, please! Does anyone wish to make any remarks?

PETER. Mr Chairman.

ASL. The Mayor will address the meeting.

PETER. In consideration of the close relationship in which, as you all know, I stand to the present Medical Officer of the Baths, I should have preferred not to speak this evening. But my official position with regard to the Baths and my solicitude for the vital interests of the town compel me to bring forward a motion. I venture to presume that there is not a single one of our citizens present who considers it desirable that unreliable and exaggerated accounts of the sanitary condition of the Baths and the town should be spread abroad.

SEVERAL VOICES. No, no! Certainly not! We protest against it!

PETER. Therefore I should like to propose that the meeting should not permit the Medical Officer either to read or comment on his proposed lecture.

95

DR STO. [*impatiently.*] Not permit—! What the devil—!

MRS STO. [*coughing.*] Ahem!—ahem!

DR STO. [*collecting himself.*] Very well. Go ahead!

PETER. In my communication to the "People's Messenger," I have put the essential facts before the public in such a way that every fair-minded citizen can easily form his own opinion. From it you will see that the main result of the Medical Officer's proposals—apart from their·constituting a vote of censure on the leading men of the town—would be to saddle the ratepayers with an unnecessary expenditure of at least some thousands of pounds.

[*Sounds of disapproval among the audience, and some cat-calls.*]

Why is Aslaksen's support of Peter so well received?

ASL. [*ringing his bell.*] Silence, please, gentlemen! I beg to support the Mayor's motion. I quite agree with him that there is something behind this agitation started by the Doctor. He talks about the Baths; but it is a revolution he is aiming at—he wants to get the administration of the town put into new hands. No one doubts the honesty of the Doctor's intentions—no one will suggest that there can be any two opinions as to that. I myself am a believer in self-government for the people, provided it does not fall too heavily on the rate-payers. But that would be the case here; and that is why I will see Dr Stockmann damned—I beg your pardon—before I go with him in the matter. You can pay too dearly for a thing sometimes; that is my opinion.

[*Loud applause on all sides.*]

Hovstad presents himself as the representative of the crowd. He accuses Dr Stockmann of being swayed by his heart rather than by his head. Is this true of Hovstad himself? If so, how will he deliver his speech?

HOV. I, too, feel called upon to explain my position. Dr Stockmann's agitation appeared to be gaining a certain amount of sympathy at first, so I supported it as impartially as I could. But presently we had reason to suspect that we had allowed ourselves to be misled by misrepresentation of the state of affairs—

DR STO. Misrepresentation—!

96

Hovstad uses some common public speaking techniques. His third speech contains rhetorical questions. What is the effect of this?
How does he make the most of these questions? What is the effect of the repetition in his fourth speech? Work to create a rhythm from the repetition.
How does Hovstad's speech affect Dr Stockmann? Dr Stockmann's family? If Hovsted indicates the family by a gesture, how might each of them react?

HOV. Well, let us say a not entirely trustworthy representation. The Mayor's statement has proved that. I hope no one here has any doubts as to my liberal principles; the attitude of the "People's Messenger" towards important political questions is well known to every one. But the advice of experienced and thoughtful men has convinced me that in purely local matters a newspaper ought to proceed with a certain caution.

ASL. I entirely agree with the speaker.

HOV. And, in the matter before us, it is now an undoubted fact that Dr Stockmann has public opinion against him. Now, what is an editor's first and most obvious duty, gentlemen? Is it not to work in harmony with his readers? Has he not received a sort of tacit mandate to work persistently and assiduously for the welfare of those whose opinions he represents? Or is it possible I am mistaken in that?

VOICES FROM THE CROWD. No, no! You are quite right!

HOV. It has cost me a severe struggle to break with a man in whose house I have been lately a frequent guest—a man who till to-day has been able to pride himself on the undivided good-will of his fellow-citizens—a man whose only, or at all events whose essential, failing is that he is swayed by his heart rather than his head.

A FEW SCATTERED VOICES. That is true! Bravo, Stockmann!

HOV. But my duty to the community obliged me to break with him. And there is another consideration that impels me to oppose him, and, as far as possible, to arrest him on the perilous course he has adopted; that is, consideration for his family—

DR STO9 Please stick to the water-supply and drainage!

HOV. —consideration, I repeat, for his wife and his children for whom he has made no provision.

MOR. Is that us, mother?

Section Seven

What effect does Dr Stockmann's opening speech have on Peter? on the crowd? How confident is his manner? How does this affect his speech?

How well does the crowd understand Dr Stockmann's position?

What does Peter's reaction to the doctor's accusation suggest?

MRS STO.   Hush!

ASL.   I will now put the Mayor's proposition to the vote.

DR STO.   There is no necessity! To-night I have no intention of dealing with all that filth down at the Baths. No; I have something quite different to say to you.

PETER.   [aside.]   What is coming now?

A DRUNKEN MAN.   [by the entrance door.] I am a ratepayer! And therefore I have a right to speak too! And my entire—firm—inconceivable opinion is—

A NUMBER OF VOICES.   Be quiet, at the back there! *Others.*   He is drunk! Turn him out! [*They turn him out.*]

DR STO.   Am I allowed to speak?

ASL.   [*ringing his bell.*]   Dr Stockmann will address the meeting.

DR STO.   I should like to have seen anyone, a few days ago, dare to attempt to silence me as has been done to-night! I would have defended my sacred rights as a man, like a lion! But now it is all one to me; I have something of even weightier importance to say to you.

[*The crowd presses nearer to him,* MORTEN KIIL *conspicuous among them.*]

PETER.   [*with a cough.*]   Ahem!

DR STO.   I will impart to you a discovery of a far wider scope than the trifling matter that our water-supply is poisoned and our medicinal Baths are standing on pestiferous soil.

A NUMBER OF VOICES.   [*shouting.*]   Don't talk about the Baths! We won't hear you! None of that!

DR STO.   I have already told you that what I want to speak about is the great discovery I have made lately—the discovery that all the sources of our *moral* life are poisoned and that the whole fabric of our civic community is founded on the pestiferous soil of falsehood.

VOICES OF DISCONCERTED CITIZENS9   What is that he says?

PETER.   Such an insinuation—!

Dr Stockmann is sincere in what he is saying. He has been the servant of the people.

How is his manner of delivery different from that of the previous speakers?

There is some variety in the reaction of the crowd to Dr Stockmann. Work to show this during the growing alienation and uproar as Dr Stockmann warms to the attack. Discipline the presentation of the lack of control in the meeting—know what is happening, when it happens, and who makes it happen.

ASL. [*with his hand on his bell.*] I call upon the speaker to moderate his language.

DR STO. I have always loved my native town as a man only can love the home of his youthful days. I was not old when I went away from here and exile, longing and memories cast as it were an additional halo over both the town and its inhabitants. [*Some clapping and applause.*] and there I stayed, for many years, in a horrible hole far away up north. When I came into contact with some of the people that lived scattered about among the rocks, I often thought it would of been more service to the poor half-starved creatures if a veterinary doctor had been sent up there, instead of a man like me. [*Murmurs among the crowd.*]

BILL. [*laying down his pen.*] I'm damned if I have ever heard—!

HOV. It is an insult to a respectable population!

DR STO. Wait a bit! I do not think anyone will charge me with having forgotten my native town up there. I was like one of the eider-ducks brooding on its nest, and what I hatched was—the plans for these Baths. [*Applause and protests.*] and then when fate at last decreed for me the great happiness of coming home again—I assure you, gentlemen, I thought I had nothing more in the world to wish for. Or rather, there was one thing I wished for—eagerly, untiringly, ardently—and that was to be able to be of service to my native town and the good of the community.

PETER. [*looking at the ceiling.*] You chose a strange way of doing it—ahem!

DR STO. And so, with my eyes blinded to the real facts, I revelled in happiness. But yesterday morning I realised the colossal stupidity of the authorities—. [*Uproar, shouts and laughter.* MRS STOCKMANN *coughs persistently.*]

PETER. Mr Chairman!

ASL. [*ringing his bell.*] By virtue of my authority—!

DR STO. It is a petty thing to catch me up on a word, Mr Aslasken. What I mean is only that I got scent of the unbelievable piggishness our leading men had been responsible for down at the Baths. I can't stand leading men at any price!—I have had enough of such people in my time. They stand in a free man's way, whichever way he turns, and what I should like best would be to see them exterminated like any other vermin—.

[*Uproar.*]

PETER. Mr Chairman, can we allow such expressions to pass?

ASL. [*with his hand on his bell.*]doctor—!

DR STO. I cannot understand how it is that I have only now acquired a clear conception of what there gentry are, when I had almost daily before my eyes in this town such an excellent specimen of them—my brother Peter—slow-witted and hide-bound in prejudice—. [*Laughter, uproar and hisses.* MRS STOCKMANN *sits coughing assiduously.* ASLAKSEN *rings his bell violently.*]

THE DRUNKEN MAN. [*who has got in again.*] Is it me he is talking about? My name's Petersen, all right—but devil take me if I—

ANGRY VOICES. Turn out that drunken man! Turn him out. [*He is turned out again.*]

PETER. Who was that person?

1ST CITIZEN. I don't know who he is, Mr Mayor.

2ND CITIZEN. He doesn't belong here.

3RD CITIZEN. I expect he is a navvy from over at [*the rest is inaudible.*]

ASL. He had obviously had too much beer.— Proceed, Doctor, but please strive to be moderate in your language.

DR STO. Very well, gentlemen, I will say no more about our leading men. I cherish the comforting conviction that these parasites—all these venerable relics of a dying school of thought— are most admirably paving the way for their own extinction; they need no doctor's help to hasten their end. It is not they who are the most dangerous enemies of truth and freedom amongst us.

SHOUTS FROM ALL SIDES. Who then? Who is it? Name! Name!

DR STO. You may depend upon it I shall name them! That is precisely the great discovery I made yesterday. [*Raises his voice.*] The most dangerous enemy to truth and freedom amongst us is the compact majority—yes, the damned compact Liberal majority—that is it! Now you know; [*Tremendous uproar. Most of the crowd are shouting, stamping and hissing. Some of the older men among them exchange stolen glances and seem to be enjoying themselves.* MRS STOCK-MANN *gets up, looking anxious.* EJLIF *and* MORTEN *advance threateningly upon some schoolboys who are playing pranks.* ASLAKSEN *rings his bell and begs for silence.* HOVSTAD *and* BILLING *both talk at once, but are inaudible. At last quiet is restored.*]

ASL. As chairman, I call upon the speaker to withdraw the ill-considered expressions he has just used.

DR STO. Never, Mr Aslaksen! It is the majority in our community that denies me my freedom and seeks to prevent my speaking the truth.

HOV. The majority always has right on its side.

BILL. And truth too, by God!

DR STO. The majority *never* has right on its side. Never, I say! That is one of these social lies against which an independent, intelligent man must wage war. Who is it that constitute the majority of the population in a country? Is it the clever folk or the stupid?—you can never pretend that it is right that the stupid folk should govern the clever ones! [*Uproar and cries.*] Oh, yes—you can shout me down, I know! but you cannot answer me. The majority has *might* on its side—unfortunately; but *right* it has *not*. I am in the right—I and a few other scattered individuals. The minority is always in the right. [*Renewed uproar.*]

HOV. So the Doctor is a revolutionary now!

DR STO. Good heavens—of course I am, Mr Hovstad! I propose to raise a revolution against the lie that the majority has the monopoly of the truth.

ASL. It appears to me that the speaker is wandering a long way from his subject.

PETER. I quite agree with the Chairman.

DR STO. Have you gone clean out of your senses, Peter? I am sticking as closely to my subject as I can; for my subject is precisely this, that it is the masses, the majority—this infernal compact majority—that poisons the sources of our moral life and infects the ground we stand on.

HOV. And all this because the great, broad-minded majority of the people is prudent enough to show deference only to well-ascertained and well-approved truths?

DR STO. Ah, my good Mr Hovstad, don't talk nonsense about well-ascertained truths! The truths of which the masses now approve are the very truths that the fighters at the outposts held to in the days of our grandfathers.

HOV. But instead of standing there using vague generalities, it would be interesting if you would tell us what these old truths are.

[Applause from many quarters.]

DR STO. Oh, I could give you a whole string of such abominations; but to begin with I will confine myself to one well-approved truth, which at bottom is a foul lie, but upon which nevertheless Mr Hovstad and the "People's Messenger" and all the "Messenger's" supporters are nourished.

HOV. And that is—?

DR STO. That is, that the common folk, the ignorant and incomplete element in the community, have the same right to pronounce judgment and to approve, to direct and to govern, as the isolated, intellectually superior personalities in it.

BILL. Well, damn me if ever I—

HOV. [at the same time, shouting out.] Fellow-citizens, take good note of that!

A NUMBER OF VOICES. [angrily.] Oho!—we are not the People! Only the superior folk are to govern, are they!

A WORKMAN.   Turn the fellow out, for talking such rubbish!

ANOTHER.   Out with him!

ANOTHER.   [*calling out.*] Blow your horn, Evensen!

[*A horn is blown loudly, amidst hisses and an angry uproar.*]

DR STO. [*when the noise has somewhat abated.*] Be reasonable! I don't in the least expect you to agree with me all at once; but I must say I did expect Mr Hovstad to admit I was right, when he had recovered his composure a little. He claims to be a freethinker—

VOICES. [*in murmurs of astonishment.*] Free-thinker, did he say? Is Hovstad a freethinker?

HOV. [*shouting.*] Prove it, Dr Stockmann! When have I said so in print?

DR STO. [*reflecting.*] No, confound it, you are right!—you have never had the courage to. Well, I won't put you in a hole, Mr Hovstad. Let us say it is I that am the freethinker, then. I am going to prove to you, scientifically, that the "People's Messenger" leads you by the nose in a shameful manner when it tells you that you—that the common people, the crowd, the masses, are the real essence of the People. That is only a newspaper lie, I tell you! The common people are nothing more than the raw material of which a People is made. [*Groans, laughter and uproar.*] Well, isn't that the case? Isn't there an enormous difference between a well-bred and an ill-bred strain of animals? Or take the case of dogs, with whom we humans are on such intimate terms. Think first of an ordinary common cur—I mean one of the horrible, coarse-haired, low-bred curs that do nothing but run about the streets and befoul the walls of the houses. Compare one of these curs with a poodle whose sires for many generations have been bred in a gentleman's house, where they have had the best of food and had the opportunity of hearing soft voices and music. Do you not think that the poodle's brain is developed to quite a different degree from that of the cur? Of course it is. It is puppies of well-bred poodles like that, that showmen train to do incredibly clever tricks—things that a common cur could never learn to do even if it stood on its head. [*Uproar and mocking cries.*]

A CITIZEN. [*calls out.*] Are you going to make out we are dogs, now?

ANOTHER CITIZEN. We are not animals, Doctor!

DR STO. Yes, but, bless my soul, we *are*, my friend! It is true we are the finest animals anyone could wish for; but, even amongst us, exceptionally fine animals are rare. There is a tremendous difference between poodle-men and cur-men. And the amusing part of it is, that Mr Hovstad quite agrees with me as long as it is a question of four-footed animals—

HOV. Yes, it is true enough as far as they are concerned.

DR STO. Very well. But as soon as I extend the principle and apply it to two-legged animals, Mr Hovstad stops short. He no longer dares to think independently, or to pursue his ideas to their logical conclusion; so he turns the whole theory upside down and proclaims in the "People's Messenger" that it is the street curs that are the finest specimens in the menagerie.

HOV. I lay no claim to any sort of distinction. I am the son of humble countryfolk, and I am proud that the stock I come from is rooted deep among the common people he insults.

VOICES. Bravo, Hovstad! Bravo! Bravo!

DR STO. The kind of common people I mean are not only to be found low down in the social scale; they crawl and swarm all around us—even in the highest social positions. You have only to look at your own fine, distinguished Mayor! My brother Peter is every bit as plebeian as anyone that walks in two shoes— [*laughter and hisses*].

PETER. I protest against personal allusions of this kind.

DR STO. [*imperturbably.*] —and that, not because he is, like myself, descended from some old rascal of a pirate from Pomerania or thereabouts—because that is who we are descended from—

PETER. An absurd legend. I deny it!

DR STO. —but because he thinks what his superiors think and holds the same opinions as they. People who do that are, intellectually speaking, common people; and that is why my magnificent brother Peter is in reality so very far from any distinction—and consequently also so far from being liberal-minded.

PETER. Mr Chairman—!

HOV. So it is only the distinguished men that are liberal-minded in this country? We are learning something quite new! [*Laughter.*]

DR STO. Yes, that is part of my new discovery too. And another part of it is that broadmindedness is almost precisely the same thing as morality. That is why I maintain that it is absolutely inexcusable in the "People's Messenger" to proclaim, day in and day out, the false doctrine that it is the masses, the crowd, the compact majority, that have the monopoly of broad-mindedness and morality—and that vice and corruption and every kind of intellectual depravity are the result of culture, just as the filth that is draining into our Baths is the result of the tanneries up at Mölledal! [*Uproar and interruptions.* DR STOCKMANN *is undisturbed, and goes on, carried away by his ardour, with a smile.*] And yet this same "People's Messenger" can go on preaching that the masses ought to be elevated to higher conditions of life!

A CITIZEN. I move that the Chairman direct the speaker to sit down.

VOICES. [*angrily.*] Hear, hear! Quite right! Make him sit down!

DR STO. [*losing his self-control.*] Then I will go and shout the truth at every street corner! I will write it in other towns' newspapers! The whole country shall know what is going on here. ·

HOV. It almost seems as if Dr Stockmann's intentions were to ruin the town.

Section Nine

Dr Stockmann refuses to withdraw his remarks. What he says and how he says it antagonise the crowd.

What are his prominent characteristics here?

How is his wife reacting?

Use what the characters say. For example, Dr Stockmann mentions that he hoped Hovsted would agree when he has "recovered his composure a little". This indicates Hovstad's emotional state.

Section Ten

Dr Stockmann loses his self-control, and therefore any ability to control the audience. His fervour isolates him even from his wife.

105

Where is he standing now?

Chairman Aslaksen takes over the leadership.

What is the effect on the meeting of formalising the procedure?

Peter leaves. How might he indicate his attitude to Dr Stockmann before leaving?

DR STO.   Yes, my native town is so dear to me that I would rather ruin it than see it flourishing upon a lie.

ASL.   This is really serious. [*Uproar and cat-calls.* MRS STOCKMANN *coughs, but to no purpose; her husband does not listen to her any longer.*]

HOV.   [*shouting above the din.*]   A man must be a public enemy to wish to ruin a whole community!

DR STO.   [*with growing fervour.*]   What does the destruction of a community matter, I tell you! All who live by lies ought to be exterminated like vermin! You will end by infecting the whole country; you will bring about such a state of things that the whole country will deserve to be ruined.

VOICES FROM THE CROWD.   That is talking like an out-and-out enemy of the people!

BILL.   There sounded the voice of the people, by all that's holy!

THE WHOLE CROWD.   [*shouting.*]   Yes, yes! He is an enemy of the people! He hates his country! He hates his own people!

ASL.   Both as a citizen and as an individual, I am profoundly disturbed by what we have had to listen to. Dr Stockmann has shown himself in a light I should never have dreamed of. I am unhappily obliged to subscribe to the opinion which I have just heard my estimable fellow-citizens utter; and I propose that we should give expression to that opinion in a resolution. I propose a resolution as follows: "This meeting declares that it considers Dr Thomas Stockmann, Medical Officer of the Baths, to be an enemy of the people." [*A storm of cheers and applause. A number of men surround the* DOCTOR *and hiss him.* MRS STOCKMANN *and* PETRA *have got up from their seats.* MORTEN *and* EJLIF *are fighting the other schoolboys for hissing; some of their elders separate them.*]

DR STO.   [*to the men who are hissing him.*] Oh, you fools! I tell you that—

The resolution concerning Dr Stockmann is serious. What is the core of the discussion of the citizens as they prepare to vote? What is its effect on Dr Stockmann?

ASL. [*ringing his bell.*] We cannot hear you now, Doctor. A formal vote is about to be taken; but, out of regard for personal feelings, it shall be by ballot and not verbal. Have you any clean paper, Mr Billing?

BILL. I have both blue and white here.

ASL. [*going to him.*] That will do nicely; we shall get on more quickly that way. Cut it up into small strips—yes, that's it. [*To the meeting.*] Blue means no; white means yes. I will come round myself and collect votes.

[PETER STOCKMANN *leaves the hall.* ASLAKSEN *and one or two others go around the room with the slips of paper in their hats.*]

1ST CITIZEN. [*to* HOVSTAD.] I say, what has come to the Doctor? What are we to think of it?

HOV. Oh, you know how headstrong he is.

2ND CITIZEN. [*to* BILLING.] Billing, you go to their house—have you ever noticed if the fellow drinks?

BILL. Well I'm hanged if I know what to say. There are always spirits on the table when you go.

3RD CITIZEN. I rather think he goes quite off his head sometimes.

1ST CITIZEN. I wonder if there is any madness in his family?

BILL. I shouldn't wonder if there were.

4TH CITIZEN. No, it is nothing more than sheer malice; he wants to get even with somebody for something or other.

BILL. Well certainly he suggested a rise in his salary on one occasion lately, and did not get it.

THE CITIZENS. [*together.*] Ah!—then it is easy to understand how it is!

THE DRUNKEN MAN. [*who has got amongst the audience again.*] I want a blue one, I do! And I want a white one too!

VOICES. It's that drunken chap again! Turn him out!

Section Eleven

What is Morten Kiil's motive in speaking to Dr Stockmann?

MORTEN KIIL. [*going up to* DR STOCKMANN.] Well, Stockmann, do you see what these monkey tricks of yours lead to?

What does the interaction reveal about Dr Stockmann? about the opposition of which Morten Kiil is a member?
How can the focus remain on the speakers rather than the crowd while the organisation of the ballot goes on in this and the following unit.

Section Twelve

The stout man indicates repercussions. How does the conversation affect the Stockmanns?

Section Thirteen

Aslaksen announces the result. Work on the repetition of cheering and applause to help build the tone of the meeting.

DR STO. I have done my duty.

MORTEN KIIL. What was that you said about the tanneries at Mölledal?

DR STO. You heard well enough. I said they were the source of all the filth.

MORTEN KIIL. My tannery too?

DR STO. Unfortunately your tannery is by far the worst.

MORTEN KIIL. Are you going to put that in the papers?

DR STO. I shall conceal nothing.

MORTEN KIIL. That may cost you dear, Stockmann. [*goes out.*]

A STOUT MAN. [*going up to* CAPTAIN HORSTER, *without taking any notice of the ladies.*] Well, Captain, so you lend your house to enemies of the people?

HORS. I imagine I can do what I like with my own possessions, Mr Vik.

THE STOUT MAN. Then you can have no objection to my doing the same with mine.

HORS. What do you mean, sir?

THE STOUT MAN. You shall hear from me in the morning. [*Turns his back on him and moves off.*]

PETRA. Was that not your owner, Captain Horster?

HORS. Yes, that was Mr Vik the ship-owner.

ASL. [*with the voting-papers in his hands, gets up on to the platform and rings his bell.*] Gentlemen, allow me to announce the result. By the votes of every one here except one person—

A YOUNG MAN. That is the drunk chap!

ASL. By the votes of every one here except a tipsy man, this meeting of citizens declares Dr Thomas Stockmann to be an enemy of the people. [*Shouts and applause.*] Three cheers for our ancient and honourable citizen community! [*Renewed applause.*] Three cheers for our able and energetic Mayor, who has so loyally suppressed the promptings of family feeling! [*Cheers*] The meeting is dissolved. [*Gets down.*]

BILL. Three cheers for the Chairman!

Section Fourteen

The mood of the crowd changes again. What provokes the change?
Dr Stockmann exits.
How do you show he is not running away? Contrast his exit with that of his family and with that of the people.

In sections twelve and thirteen the threat to Dr Stockmann was in words. Build the noise and the movement to make a strong ending—perhaps the threat of physical violence.

THE WHOLE CROWD.   Three cheers for Aslaksen! Hurrah!

DR STO.   My hat and coat, Petra! Captain, have you room on your ship for passengers to the New World?

HORS.   For you and yours we will make room, Doctor.

DR STO.   [as PETRA *helps him into his coat.*] Good. Come, Katherine! Come, boys!

MRS STO.   [*in an undertone.*] Thomas, dear, let us go out by the back way.

DR STO.   No back ways for me, Katherine. [*Raising his voice.*] You will hear more of this enemy of the people, before he shakes the dust off his shoes upon you! I am not so forgiving as a certain Person; I do not say: "I forgive you, for ye know not what ye do."

ASL.   [*shouting.*]   That is a blasphemous comparison, Dr Stockmann!

BILL.   It is, by God. It's dreadful for an earnest man to listen to.

A COARSE VOICE.   Threatens us now, does he!

OTHER VOICES.   [*excitedly.*]   Let's go and break his windows! Duck him in the fjord!

ANOTHER VOICE.   Blow your horn, Evensen! Pip, pip!

[*Horn-blowing, hisses, and wild cries.* DR STOCKMANN *goes out through the hall with his family,* HORSTER *elbowing a way for them.*]

THE WHOLE CROWD.   [*howling after as they go.*]   Enemy of the People! Enemy of the People!

BILL.   [*as he puts his papers together.*]   Well, I'm damned if I go and drink toddy with the Stockmanns tonight!

[*The crowd press towards the exit. The uproar continues outside; shouts of "Enemy of the People!" are heard from without.*]